GOD'S CONSTANT PRESENCE
True Stories of Everyday Miracles

Angels & Divine Encounters

GOD'S CONSTANT PRESENCE
True Stories of Everyday Miracles

Angels & Divine Encounters

EDITORS OF GUIDEPOSTS

Guideposts

A Gift from Guideposts

Thank you for your purchase! We appreciate your support and want to express our gratitude with a special gift just for you.

Dive into *Spirit Lifters*, a complimentary booklet that will fortify your faith and offer solace during challenging moments. It contains 31 carefully selected verses from scripture that will soothe your soul and uplift your spirit.

Please use the QR code or go to **guideposts.org/spiritlifters** to download.

Angels & Divine Encounters

Published by Guideposts
100 Reserve Road, Suite E200
Danbury, CT 06810
Guideposts.org

Copyright © 2025 by Guideposts. All rights reserved.

This book, or parts thereof, may not be reproduced, stored in a retrieval system, or transmitted in any form or by any means, electronic, mechanical, photocopying, recording or otherwise, without the written permission of the publisher.

Cover design by Serena Fox Design Company
Interior design by Serena Fox Design Company
Cover photo by LeQuangNhut/Shutterstock
Typeset by Aptara, Inc.

ISBN 978-1-961251-75-5 (hardcover)
ISBN 978-1-961251-76-2 (softcover)
ISBN 978-1-961251-77-9 (epub)

Printed and bound in the United States of America
10 9 8 7 6 5 4 3 2 1

See, I am sending an angel ahead of you to guard you along the way and to bring you to the place I have prepared. Pay attention to him and listen to what he says.

—*Exodus 23:20-21 (NIV)*

TABLE *of* CONTENTS

Introduction.......................... 1
    God's Countless Messengers

Chapter 1........................... 11
    Angel Encounters

Chapter 2........................... 53
    Mysterious Strangers

Chapter 3........................... 87
    Guarded by Invisible Angels

Chapter 4.......................... 115
    God Sends His Comfort

Chapter 5.......................... 149
    Miracle Moments

Chapter 6.......................... 175
    Visions and Messages from God

Chapter 7.......................... 209
    God's Human Angels

Contributors 244

Acknowledgments 245

God's Countless Messengers
Tez Brooks

"I SEE A HUGE angel behind you, brother!" the preacher said as he finished praying for me.

The hair stood on the back of my neck. I opened my eyes and looked directly at the pastor, but in my peripheral vision, I could see broad, muscular shoulders behind me—so massive they extended on both sides, a foot beyond my own frame.

Without turning around, I perceived from the corner of my eye that this heavenly being was dressed in ancient battle armor, sporting a helmet and a coat of mail.

I wept with gratitude.

God was showing His deep love and care for me by sending this warrior in my time of need. I was in the middle of a horrible divorce and custody dispute. I needed to know the Lord was in my corner, fighting for me. Now, this angel appeared and the dark hopelessness enveloping my heart and mind disappeared as peace swept over me. I knew I was protected. I walked away encouraged and faith-filled.

In the unseen realms of this universe dwell invisible, powerful heavenly beings. They travel back and forth from heaven to earth, fulfilling their Master's assignments. Whether it's saving the smallest of toddlers from falling down a flight of stairs or directing political affairs of entire countries, they bullet through the atmosphere to direct, protect, and engage in battle. They are angels, and one might be standing beside you even as you read this.

More than half of the books of the Bible talk about them, and the word "angel" appears more than 250 times in Scripture. We can safely say these beings have had a significant role in history. They are not mythological creatures like the Greek god Zeus or the Easter Bunny. If you genuinely believe the Bible is God's holy, living Word, spoken to all of humanity, indisputably accurate and reliable, then you, too, believe angels exist and carry out a wonderful ministry.

Over the centuries, poets and songwriters have written about them, theater and film have portrayed them, and people of all types have testified to sensing their presence. But what exactly *are* they, and why do they exist?

What Are Angels?

I DON'T WANT to turn this into a Bible study by providing so many scriptures it's overwhelming. But I encourage you to study the topic on your own, relying on the knowledge contained in God's Word rather than pop music or Hollywood. Nowhere does the Bible lead us to believe that we become angels when we die. And the cherubim described within are definitely not cute little naked babies with bows and arrows. We don't even know for sure if all angels have wings.

So, what does Scripture reveal about these creatures?

Sometimes called "sons of God," angels are created spiritual beings with moral judgment and high intelligence. They are supernatural or beyond the laws of nature; unless they manifest themselves to us, they are invisible to the human eye. Unlike

God, they are finite and can't be everywhere at once or read our minds. But there are a whole lot of them—we have no idea how many.

I've wondered what it would be like if I were responsible for hiring a personal guardian angel. What job requirements would I list in a help-wanted ad?

> *WANTED: GUARDIAN ANGEL. Must be strong and agile. Able to lift cars and stop bullets. Willing to appear in human form as needed. Military training required. Millennia of experience preferred but not necessary. Please provide a list of demons slain. Room and board provided.*

I suspect the ad would not go to the heavenly hosts but directly to God. After all, He is the one who created them and delegates their assignments.

God created angels (Nehemiah 9:6; Psalm 148:2, 5), and they obviously exercise their own moral will, because many angels decided to follow Lucifer in a coup against God (Jude 1:6)—which didn't go well for them (Revelation 12:3–9). Among the activities that we find angels performing in Scripture are communicating with humans, singing, and playing instruments. We see this often, as for example when angels sing at Jesus's birth (Luke 2:13–14) or play a trumpet (Revelation 8:6ff). They have more power and greater abilities than us, because we read in the Old Testament of one angel killing thousands of people at once (2 Kings 19:35). Often, humans have been fearful when they meet these beings, falling face down at the sight of them. Angels of death and plagues are mentioned in both Old and New Testaments, so no wonder many were frightened of them.

We *do* know that these holy ones were not made in God's image like us, and they are not as loved by God as humans. He doesn't save angels (Hebrews 2:16), but He died in our place to ensure our souls receive redemption.

That's humbling when you realize the power angels hold and their proven loyalty to God. I often wonder if they tilt their heads in curiosity when we talk about God's amazing grace or how His love lifted us from the depths of sin. Do they shake their heads in disbelief when we demonstrate a lack of faith? They have no idea what it feels like to fall so often, yet to experience God's forgiveness, the way that humans do.

What Angels Do

THERE IS NO DEBATING these watchers carry job titles with specific functions. The Bible speaks of some that are called angels (Luke 2:13) while others are cherubim (Genesis 3:24), seraphim (Isaiah 6:2–7), and living creatures (Revelation 4:6–8). Some, like Michael the archangel, hold high military rank and may command lesser angels (Daniel 10:10–14, 21). Gabriel's role seems to be that of a messenger because when he appears in Scripture, he is delivering critical information (Daniel 8:16ff; Luke 1:19, 26).

There are serving angels like those who ministered to Jesus in the wilderness (Matthew 4:11). There are patrolling angels and guardians, too (Psalm 91:11–12). Although we never see proof in Scripture that guardian angels are assigned to one human all their life, we hear of many who have encountered mysterious strangers appearing in human form and then vanishing (Hebrews 13:2).

One such witness was described in Douglas Connelly's book *Angels Standing Guard*. The incident happened in 1988, when a missionary named Esther Mass was on her way to church. Not far from her home, she was in an automobile accident. Immediately, a man in his thirties appeared at her car door, taking Esther's hand and comforting her. A peace overwhelmed her. He turned and asked a bystander to call 911.

"What is your name, sir?" Esther said.

"I can't tell you my name, but you will be fine."

As soon as the emergency vehicle arrived, he disappeared.

Can we say for sure that this was an angel? No, but it fits with what we know in Scripture about how God delegates His care through them (Hebrews 1:14).

Other stories I have heard over the years mention unusually tall men who give wise counsel or advice, or who know something about a person they would have no earthly way of knowing.

Ed, a pastor friend of mine, had two men like this approach and sit with him at a café while he ate his meal. They ordered nothing, but encouraged him in his ministry and told him to continue serving the Lord in spite of the opposition he'd been experiencing.

"Be blessed, Edwin," one said as they stood up.

"Go with our Lord, Redeemed One," said the other as he shook Ed's hand.

Weird way to say goodbye, Ed thought.

They had no way of knowing Ed's birthname was Edwin. It could just as well have been Edward, Edgar, or Edmund. My pastor friend was indeed going through a time of significant opposition from a few power-hungry, disgruntled parishioners who didn't appreciate Edwin's leadership style. The situation had gotten so bad that he was thinking about resigning.

When Ed pulled himself together, he turned around in his seat to watch them leave. The large picture windows on either side of the front door offered an unobstructed view of passersby walking in either direction.

Ed never saw the men walk in either direction. He kept watching, assuming they had stopped momentarily in front of the door. When a woman entered the café, the open door showed no one standing in the doorway.

The strangers had vanished.

This was a common thing in Scripture, too—heavenly visitors appearing as human travelers. One example is when angels appeared to Abraham and then to his nephew, Lot (Genesis 18, 19). Another story in the book of Acts shows us how God used angels to reveal His will in the midst of human stubbornness. The Lord wanted to give the early Christians guidance when they were not seeking it.

These ancient believers in the Jewish community were pretty content to keep the gospel confined to their own people. But God's burden was for the entire world to hear the message of Christ. So, God began to move his people in new and unexpected directions—using angels to open the door.

In one case, an angel appeared to Philip, telling him to go south down a desert road (Acts 8:26–40). So, he did, and ran into an Ethiopian official who was reading Scripture. Philip ends up helping this non-Jewish man understand the passage and goes on to explain the good news of Jesus. The man believes, so Philip baptizes him. God delegated an angel to show Philip that salvation was for all humans, not just his chosen people, the Jews.

My favorite Bible story of an angel is when Peter was rescued from prison (Acts 12). A rescuing angel shows up in Peter's jail cell and wakes him with a slap. For real—read it for yourself. He causes Peter's chains to drop off and says, "Hurry up! Get your clothes on and follow me out of here."

The prison gates open on their own accord, and as they walk past the guards, Peter thinks he's dreaming all this. They get out on the street and the angel just disappears without so much as a goodbye! Peter later finds out his friends had been praying for him, and that's why the angel delivered him.

What an unbelievable miracle! I'm not sure I'd be so calm if an angel slapped me while I was sleeping. But I love the audacity of this angel, who waltzes Peter right past the guard station as if he were merely a visitor and then leaves him out on the street to find his way home.

Did this impatient, no-nonsense heavenly rescuer have a busy schedule that night? Or had he done this so much that he was just "in the zone?" I'm not sure, but I like him!

Chances are you've heard modern-day accounts of hitchhikers from heaven or mysterious rescuers. Some stories are passed on from person to person, with the details so altered it's impossible to determine their accuracy. But what you hold in your hands are eyewitness reports of modern encounters with these beings, along with many other stories of God's intervention and protection in people's lives.

I want to be more receptive to the work of angels in my life. I am grateful for these mighty servants and long to "show hospitality to strangers" (Hebrews 13:2, NIV) more fully. The more I study what God's Word says about angels, the more I wonder how many times I have taken credit for something they did.

- My defensive driving through New York City.
- My ability to find a location without a GPS.
- My expert swimming skills in a riptide.
- My keen discernment to share the gospel with an unbeliever.

- The agility to land on my feet when I missed the ladder's last rung.
- Walking in on a grease fire just in time to smother it.
- Pulling away from a saw blade just in time to save my thumb.
- My professionalism to land a new job with better pay.

How arrogant of me to believe my quick thinking, youthful physical condition, keen communication skills, or even a fresh haircut saved me from embarrassment, harm, or disaster. Who am I kidding? I barely remember to take my ginkgo biloba!

As you read about the angel encounters in this book, remember to explore what Scripture has to say. Understand that these celestial workers serve many purposes. Much like an army, God gives them levels of authority over one another. Some are messengers; others protect us or even go to war for us. Still others bring blessings or curses, even death. Some stay around God's throne, glorifying him for eternity. Still, none of them desires to be prayed to, admired, or held in superior status (Revelation 22:8–9, Colossians 2:18). If we place too much interest in angels, we shift our attention to one of God's created beings rather than focusing on the Creator. Let us be diligent never to elevate angels to anything more than agents of God.

The holy ones that I am most curious about are the glorifying angels (Revelation 5:11–12), whose job is to stand around the throne forever, proclaiming how wonderful our God is. They cry out with a loud voice, "Worthy is the Lamb, who was slain, to receive power and wealth and wisdom and strength and honor and glory and praise!" (NIV).

How I long to be there and worship along with them forever. As it is now, during a Sunday worship service, I find myself tired of standing after only 15 minutes of praising God with the congregation. One day, I'll have a new body and won't have to worry about fatigue.

Glorifying the Creator is what this is all about—our journey with God, this book, and its stories. It's about His majesty in the end. This collection of angelic encounters is not meant to have us focus on God's messengers, but to focus on God himself. Everything angels say and do is to reflect God's glory and majesty and point us to Jesus. The events recorded on these pages are meant to encourage and strengthen, knowing the Almighty cares so much for us that He orchestrates myriads of heavenly beings to watch over His beloved children.

Seeing that huge warrior angel's appearance years ago comforted me, knowing the Lord loved me enough to send it. I'm grateful that the Almighty dispatches his helpers to watch over us.

My prayer for you, dear reader, is that you might finish this book uplifted, knowing the one true God of the Universe not only provides angelic help to live your life, but even greater than that, He sacrificed Himself so you might have a way to approach Him and have a relationship with Him. Grace to you.

> Believers, look up—take courage. The angels are nearer than you think.
>
> —Billy Graham

CHAPTER 1
Angel Encounters

A Miracle Birth 12
   Laurie Davies

An Angel in a Patrol Car 18
   Sharon Kirby

The Singing Angelic Host 23
   Betty A. Rodgers-Kulich

A Christmas Angel on the Highway 28
   Linda VanderWier

The Rubber and the Road 33
   Lorna Skylar

Angel with a Business Card 38
   Marilyn Turk

Angels on the Exit Ramp 42
   Sue McCusker

God's Heavenly Messenger 47
   Sara Etgen-Baker

A Miracle Birth
Laurie Davies

A monitor in my birthing suite blared a steady, piercing alarm, alerting medical professionals to rush into the room. My newborn son's airway was clogged. One nurse exchanged a worried look with another as the team raced against the clock trying to help him breathe. His color slipped into an alarming state of chalky blue.

"Breathe, little guy. Breathe!" one of the nurses mouthed.

Seconds turned into a minute. Watching from across the room in my hospital bed, a helpless sense of panic set in. I uttered a simple prayer.

"God, send help."

They say silence can be deafening, but this silence was deadly. Our son was running out of time.

Finally, I thought as a short, stocky man with a white doctor's coat to match his white buzz cut calmly entered the chaos. He walked past the commotion encircling our son to my bedside, where he set his sights on my husband Greg, placing his hands squarely on his shoulders. "Don't worry, I'm not the janitor," he said, oddly. And then, with eye contact so piercing that it settled—in a second—our worst fears, he said directly to my husband: "Your son is going to be OK."

He had never looked in the direction of our baby's medical bassinet.

How did he know our child was a boy?

"You gonna tell the story?" My 23-year-old son leaned across the patio table. His best friend offered a quizzical look and guided a crooked French fry into his mouth.

"Right here?" I asked.

Four lanes of traffic near our urban sidewalk table, an NBA game blaring on a dozen TVs, and the low roar of college kids talking and laughing formed an impossible soundtrack for a story as sacred as this one. We told him every year on his birthday. Sometimes he'd cry.

"Yes, here," he said. "Come on, Mom. Tell it."

His best friend's interest was piqued. He shoved his fries to the side, indicating he wanted to hear the story, too.

"OK, here goes," I said. I slurped a big gulp of water, looked at my husband, and leaned into my memories.

> **The LORD hears his people when they call to him for help. He rescues them from all their troubles.**
>
> —PSALM 34:17 (NLT)

I told our son how long his dad and I had prayed for him. How badly we had wanted a child. How we tried, and waited, and would later miscarry three other babies.

"No pressure," I joked, "but you're it, Son. Our only shot at being taken care of in our old age."

"That's going to depend on if you're buying dinner," he volleyed.

"Blackmail!" I said.

Just then I thought of a detail I'd never shared.

Thinking that now, at age 23, he was old enough to handle it, I told him about how I nicked my ankle with a razor one morning when I was pregnant with him. It was a tiny cut, but it bled freely. In a complicated pregnancy with a health condition that made every day of his development a victory, my mind went to the worst. I threw on sweats and rushed to grab my already-packed hospital bag.

"Greg, it's time," I yelled. I was 29 weeks pregnant.

My husband calmly went to the medicine cabinet and got a small bandage.

"False alarm," he said, placing the bandage on my ankle and easing me back into bed, where dreaded "bed rest" awaited. For two months already, I'd been doing my newspaper job from bed.

I got the boys up to speed on not only going to full-term in my pregnancy, but being a week overdue.

"I knew then that you'd never be a journalist like me," I said.

"I know, I know," he said retracing my now-familiar joke with a roll of his eyes. "I couldn't hit a deadline."

His friend laughed and leaned across the table, telling me with his body language to keep going.

I described the hospital room, the little baby who was turning blue, and the guy who wasn't a janitor.

"The man took his hands off your dad's shoulders, calmly walked over to you, and with a force that I thought was going to hurt you, he intubated you. He shoved that tube down your throat and you unleashed a torrent of crying and fury. And then he left the room."

And then *everyone* left the room.

"You were whisked off to the special care nursery, and your dad followed you there. My doctor finished with me and went on to see her next patient. The room was empty."

"Mom, you were by yourself? You must have been beside yourself."

"Honestly, I was just tired. You had me in labor all night long," I said, unable to resist the joke forming on my lips. "It was the first of a few sleepless nights I've had on your account."

> **For the LORD your God moves about in your camp to protect you . . .**
>
> —DEUTERONOMY 23:14 (NIV)

"Yeah, sorry about those," he said, side-glancing at his best friend, who offered his best mock *What? Who, me?* innocent face.

"But, Mom," he said. "Tell me the part you always say. The part about how it ends."

I locked eyes with my son.

"Morgan, you had a really hard time getting into this world. You were born with your airway clogged. The monitors didn't look good. Nothing looked good. But God sent someone to help and here you are. Don't ever forget—especially when times are dark and life is hard—that God must really have a special plan for your life. He worked extra to get you here."

On cue, a tear fell down my son's cheek.

I think his best friend had something in his eye, too.

Then I told them the rest of the story—my favorite part.

In hindsight, I've often wondered why the "doctor" wasn't taller. Or more commanding. Or shining with the glory of the Lord and telling two doctors, three nurses, and two terrified parents to "fear not" in a booming voice or something. Instead, he was short, stocky, and unassuming. The first words out of his mouth were to tell us he was not a janitor. He told us who he *wasn't*. And then he acted at the command of the One who was and is and is to come.

My husband got to interact with him, but I'm glad I saw and heard him, too. I think my journalistic, "get-the-facts" cynicism would have won out if my husband only relayed the experience.

Especially considering what comes next.

Almost 12 hours later, when our labor and delivery nurses came back on shift, we asked for the name of the doctor who saved our son's life. We wanted to thank him.

"A nurse intubated your son," the charge nurse said distractedly.

"No, we saw him—the doctor who forced the tube down our son's throat. He was short and stocky and older. He had a white buzz cut. What's his name?"

The nurse looked up from my chart.

"I'm sorry. No one who looks like that even has access to this floor," she said.

Again, silence—this time stunned silence—filled my birthing suite. My husband and I looked at our sleeping, *breathing* baby. We knew we had met an angel face-to-face.

Every time I visit a hospital, I look for the janitor-doctor-angel who saved our son's life. I wonder if I'll see him someday, slipping past the nurses' station on a floor he doesn't even have access to. I want to know why he made the strange janitor comment. I want him to explain the quantum mechanics of it all: Did he guide the hands of a nurse to intubate our boy? Did he insert the tube, and we were the only ones who could see it? Did God dispatch him urgently, or was he on standby for hours?

The journalist in me dies hard.

And yet my 23-year-old son lives.

So, I mostly want to see the "doctor" so I can thank him—and the One who sent him. The One who heard a simple, desperate, three-word prayer and was moved to respond.

An Angel in a Patrol Car
Sharon Kirby

My family's long trip home for the holidays could have ended in tragedy if not for the intervention of—well, I'll let you decide.

My husband, Larry, our two daughters, and I were traveling from our home in Ohio to Trenton, New Jersey, to visit his family for the Christmas holiday. In our eagerness to spend Christmas with them, we had risen early to begin the 10-hour drive. Initially we enjoyed ourselves, singing Christmas songs, talking about the special dinner we'd be sharing with the entire family, and, of course, what the kids hoped to get as presents. By the time we crossed the border into New Jersey, we were road-weary and ready to settle into the warmth and comfort of my in-laws' home.

We entered the Trenton area late at night. It was pitch dark and winter cold with a light dusting of snowflakes shrouding the road. We took the exit from the main highway and were relieved to be within 30 minutes of our destination.

Just as our excitement began to build again, a young man standing next to his car on the side of the road urgently flagged our car down. He said he was by himself and lost. Could Larry give him directions to a certain area of Trenton? Larry agreed, and suggested they move away from the off-ramp to avoid blocking any potential traffic. The young man followed us as we turned off the ramp and pulled onto the shoulder of the road.

Privately, I wondered about this man and why he would flag down an out-of-state car for directions in a local city. I didn't want to stop for that reason, but Larry saw no harm in giving the guy directions since he was from the area and knew exactly how to get him to the neighborhood he requested.

We both watched in our side mirrors as the young man's car pulled up behind us. He exited the vehicle and trotted up to speak with Larry. We were on an unlit street, and at that late hour of night, there were no other vehicles within sight. Larry turned the engine off so the young man could hear him better. I felt uneasy. *Why he would do that?* It would have been safer to leave the engine running so that we could quickly drive away in the unlikely case something untoward should happen.

> **You exalted me above my foes; from a violent man you rescued me.**
>
> —PSALM 18:48 (NIV)

As my husband spoke to the stranger, my unease only grew. Why would someone in New Jersey ask for directions from a car with Ohio license plates? While Larry was distracted by giving directions, I was staring at the car behind us, at the same time looking back at our young daughters. I saw the doors of the vehicle open, and three men suddenly exited the vehicle and began slinking up to our vehicle.

At that moment, I was terrified. Larry had not seen the others coming toward us and was trying to communicate directions to the man who flagged us down. A man who, to Larry's confusion, didn't seem to be paying much attention to the directions he was giving. My mind began racing with all the possible scenarios we could be facing. What if they attacked—or even killed—my husband? What might they do to me, to my baby girls?

Before I could warn him, a police car suddenly appeared next to us. Speaking from the driver's seat, the officer addressed my husband. "Is everything all right? Can I be of any assistance?"

> **During the night an angel of the Lord opened the doors of the jail and brought them out. "Go, stand in the temple courts," he said, "and tell the people all about this new life."**
>
> —ACTS 5:19–20 (NIV)

Larry explained that he was just giving this young man directions when the officer stopped him. "Are you from around here, sir?" he asked.

"No, I'm from Ohio, but I grew up here," Larry replied.

"You folks go on," the officer said. "I'll handle it from here."

Slightly bewildered at the officer's insistence, Larry thanked him, started the car, and began to drive off.

Unable to hold back any longer, I told him about the other men who had been approaching the car, and of my fears about what they might have intended, keeping my words cryptic to avoid frightening the girls in the back seat. He was mortified that he had not noticed the other men, nor had he realized how frightening that stop was for me.

As we spoke, Larry realized that the officer would likely be outnumbered four to one. Despite my protests, my husband

GOD'S GIFT OF SIGHT
— Tez Brooks —

THE AMERICAN ANTELOPE is the second fastest land mammal after the cheetah. Their eyesight is keen because their peripheral vision reaches an impressive 320 degrees, making it almost impossible for predators to sneak up on them. When danger approaches, they are not built to fight, but for flight. This animal models something important to Christians. Mark 13:33 reminds readers to "Be on guard! Be alert!" Believers aren't always meant to stand and fight the enemy. Often, their best chance of survival is to run—right into the arms of Jesus.

---

swung the vehicle around to return and assist the officer if necessary.

It took only seconds to return to the scene, where there was—nothing. No flashing lights, no patrol car, no officer, only the snowy tracks of two cars driving away: ours, and the one that had been parked behind us.

Larry and I looked at each other, stunned.

"I believe we have just had an angel come to our rescue," I said.

He nodded in astonishment, and we stared at each other for a moment as we processed the significance of what had just happened. We immediately thanked God for His deliverance before returning to the last leg of our journey home.

The memory of that night will never leave me—the fear of possibly being victims of a vicious crime and then being overcome by the blessing of God's loving and tangible protection.

God's Word is for us today as it was in biblical times. It tells us that God is the same yesterday, today, and forever—always. The promise of protection He gave in the Old and New Testaments remains true no matter how much time has passed. Whether the officer who rescued us was flesh and blood or of angelic nature, we have no doubt that God stepped in to protect us that night.

The Singing Angelic Host

Betty A. Rodgers-Kulich

I had never been blessed to see an angel. I'd always assumed angel appearances were for super-spiritual people, or those being assigned a special ministry. I believed sightings happened, just not to me. When I read about angel visitations in the Bible, they seemed random, never expected by the human being involved. And the appearances always caused a myriad of emotional responses in the person being visited, indicating that they were mentally and physically overwhelmed. When, to my surprise, I did have an angelic encounter, it was no different.

I was serving on a retreat for West Side Koinonia, acting as an intercessor. The purpose of a Koinonia weekend retreat is to strengthen Christians' faith walk and their bond of fellowship with other believers. I was one of twelve intercessors who prayed for the retreat and for participants in two-hour shifts. We stayed in a sequestered wing of the facility, keeping the participants unaware of our presence until it is revealed at the end. The organizers' experience is that this knowledge that there were people praying for their spiritual well-being the whole time, coming at the end of an intense retreat, makes the spiritual impact of the retreat even greater. My role in this behind-the-scenes team was covering the 2 a.m. to 4 a.m. prayer slot.

Getting up and praying at that time was a challenge. I normally need my 8 hours of sleep, but I was willing to make the sacrifice for the sake of the spiritual enrichment of others. Staying focused on the goal of loving other brothers and sisters in Christ and deepening their faith helped me to motivate myself. I prayed the participants would choose to decrease so God could increase in them, and that they would grow stronger in new fellowship with other believers.

> "He will take great delight in you; in his love he will no longer rebuke you, but will rejoice over you with singing."
>
> —ZEPHANIAH 3:17 (NIV)

During the day, when I wasn't on my shift, I had hidden behind curtains and listened to each participant as they spoke. Hearing their stories helped me to do more focused, specific prayers on their behalf when my shift came. I was privileged to overhear their encounter testimonies with Jesus, witness their transparency to other believers, and realize how they were being transformed in just a few short hours. I felt I was getting to know them better even without speaking directly to them. Now, in the early morning darkness, I focused on how I could help bring them beyond what they'd already experienced to something even higher. I wanted more for them. I wanted them eternally changed.

The last night on my shift, while everyone was asleep, I decided to go out of my sequestered area to the empty participants' meeting room to pray. As I prayed about each person at their designated seat, I asked God that they would experience

His supernatural and life-changing presence and receive everything He desired for each one. Little did I know that this work was creating an atmosphere for a heavenly visitation, and that it wouldn't be just the participants who felt the impact of my prayers.

After the first hour of my shift, once I'd finished praying for all the participants and team, I switched to quietly singing worship songs, declaring God's greatness and getting lost in His goodness. During a pause, I suddenly heard the breakfast serenade. The serenaders were a part of the team that led worship. They awakened the participants and went before them during their daily activities, leading them from one place to another, such as the meal hall or the meeting room. Now I could faintly hear the serenaders coming from the dormitories toward the meeting room.

I was bewildered. How had I prayed and worshiped so long? How had I lost track of time? I panicked, anxious about the possibility that I would be discovered by the participants—or, worse, that they'd already heard me singing. How would the team answer the questions if participants ask, "Who is she? Why haven't we seen her before?" It would ruin the surprise at the end of the retreat, when all behind-the-scenes people who had lovingly served them were revealed.

Grabbing my Bible, I started to run to our hidden rooms, hoping to escape before anyone saw me. Glancing at the clock as I went, I saw that it read 3:38 a.m. I froze. No one else should be up at this time. Who was singing?

The beautiful melodies continued, getting closer and louder, filling the meeting room in surround sound. Now that they were closer, they didn't sound like human voices. No, they were levels above any mortal choir. The fullness of the music transcended and eclipsed even the Mormon Tabernacle Choir.

Even if every person at the retreat, staff and participants, had come together to sing at this unlikely hour, they couldn't have made this beautiful sound. I knew in that moment that it had to be angelic worship and praise.

The glorious rhythm, melody, and harmonics blended with the lingering notes of my puny, insignificant worship songs, filling the room with a tangible and physical presence. The words... I couldn't comprehend them. If they were singing in a language I knew, the beauty of the sound was so intense I couldn't process the words. My mind kept repeating, *This can't be real,* yet my heart embraced it in awe and wonder. A warmth filled my heart and spread instantly throughout my body, creating a tingling sensation like electricity. I turned and fell to my knees. The sounds continued to undulate for several more minutes. Tears ran down my cheeks and I raised my hands, then bowed in wonder that I had been so fortunate to hear the angelic host.

> **And suddenly there was with the angel a multitude of the heavenly host praising God.**
>
> —LUKE 2:13–14 (NKJV)

The fear I'd experienced when I first realized the singing had no human source had been momentary. But even as I heard the singing, I understood that my own spiritual life would undergo a profound, lasting change. I was entertaining angels. I had been unaware that they had joined in until they overwhelmed my frail voice. Now the atmosphere for the participants was certainly going to be supernaturally energized. Life for all of us would never be the same.

As I walked back to my secret room, I realized sleep was not going to be necessary. I had had an encounter with heaven. The team and participants were going to come into a supernaturally activated room with the dawning of the new day. And just as I had expected, every participant was touched in profound ways as the day went on. There were salvations; one person was healed of a bad back; several people had their hearts changed after holding offenses against someone in their family. Another person had a financial breakthrough—they got notification that a debt had been forgiven. Others had their faith walk grow substantially. Jesus told Thomas, "Blessed are those who have not seen and yet have believed" (John 20:29, NIV). I am blessed because I heard, and I believe.

A Christmas Angel on the Highway

Linda VanderWier

One night, in December of 1980, I encountered someone I never dreamed I would meet.

I didn't recognize him. He wasn't famous. Not an actor, musician, politician, or sports hero. As a matter of fact, neither I nor any of the girls I was with realized at the time who we were meeting. He appeared to be an average man, perhaps approaching middle age. Nothing exceptional. We watched him and heard him speak a scant number of words, but none of us can describe anything else about him except that he drove a red pickup truck. It happened quickly and unexpectedly, but Someone besides us had obviously planned the evening long before the event took place.

I was in my last year of Bible college in Greenville, South Carolina. Christmas break dangled encouragingly only a few weeks away. Decorations were popping up everywhere on campus, and as dormitory leaders, my friends and I had the responsibility of decorating our dorm for the occasion. After spending an entire evening discussing ways to make our entryway outstandingly festive, we decided to use a live tree as a centerpiece and planned an evening to find the perfect tree.

The night arrived. All five of us climbed into the car and headed toward the lot where the Christmas trees were being sold.

The sun had set by the time we started out, with chilly weather that seemed appropriate for the occasion, adding to the gaiety.

The car seemed to bounce along the almost empty highway as we enjoyed ourselves, talking, singing, and giggling for what we thought would be an hour or two. About halfway to our destination, though, the party atmosphere quickly dampened as the car began to sputter. In all our excited planning, we had failed to check the gas gauge before leaving campus.

We rolled safely to the edge of the road and came to a stop. We were . . . nowhere. Too far to walk for help in either direction. No houses or businesses in sight. And this was before the age of cell phones. Simply put, we were in trouble. The divided road we'd been traveling was rarely busy. That night, it loomed devastatingly desolate.

We all climbed out of the car and huddled together on the side of the road. Clutching our jackets tightly, we looked back in the direction from which we hoped assistance would come. We saw two pairs of headlights on big rigs in the distance and waved our arms frantically, yelling pointlessly as they drew near. But the two oncoming semis flew unhesitatingly by.

We watched for a bit, but no other headlights appeared on the horizon. No one spoke, since no one had a clue what to do. We were stranded, we were cold, and we were frightened.

We turned back toward the gas-depleted vehicle. What we saw astonished us. An unmarked red pickup truck was parked on the side of the road about 15 yards ahead of us. It had not been there when we'd rolled off the highway. No other vehicles had passed us as we stood beside our broken-down car. Where in the world had it come from?

My heart skipped several beats as I wondered whether the person inside would prove to be a friendly stranger or someone looking to take advantage of a group of stranded girls. Who was in that truck? Male? Female? Old? Young? Good? Shady? And what did they intend to do?

The truck door opened, and a man emerged. He was slight in build. He looked to be in perhaps his 40s. Light brown hair. Blue jeans and a jacket. He glanced at us as he took a couple steps forward, and then stopped beside the bed of his truck. We watched as he silently pulled two items from the back of the truck: an empty plastic milk jug and a black siphon hose.

Never did he ask us what was wrong with our car or why we had stopped along an empty road. Any number of problems could have crippled our vehicle, but he knew what was wrong without asking. And he'd been traveling with exactly the right equipment to meet our need. As far as any of us could tell, nothing else occupied that truck bed.

We watched as he siphoned a gallon of gas out of his own tank, moving deftly, almost professionally, but never speaking. He walked past us without one word and went straight to the gas tank.

Up to that point, everything had taken place in an almost eerie silence. Finally, someone—not me!—braved up and asked him where he was from. I remember hearing his hesitation as he pointed and said, "Well, about two miles that way." He changed the direction he'd been pointing. "Well, I mean, over that direction. Actually, I'm just from around." That was it. Our entire conversation with this kind stranger ended with those few words.

> **But my God shall supply all your need according to his riches in glory by Christ Jesus.**
>
> —PHILIPPIANS 4:19 (KJV)

As he transferred the gasoline to our tank, we all thanked him. He only nodded. Someone offered to pay for the gas he had supplied. He waved his hand in dismissal, quietly shook his head, and refused any payment.

He turned and walked back to his vehicle. After placing the now-empty jug back into the truck bed, he started the truck and drove off.

That was it. The encounter ended, leaving us with a gallon of gasoline in our tank and a dozen questions in our minds.

I was the one who finally said it out loud. "Girls, I believe we've just met an angel. A real angel sent by God to help us."

> **Help us, LORD our God, for we rely on you.**
>
> —2 CHRONICLES 14:11 (NIV)

We had no other explanation. The chills I'm sure each of us experienced at that moment had nothing to do with the weather.

We soberly piled back into the car and held our breath as we waited to see if the car would restart. With what we'd just witnessed, how could we even doubt? Of course, the car started immediately. What a comforting sound to hear that engine hum again.

The incredible encounter with the gentleman God sent to rescue us so deeply impacted me that I can recall nothing else that transpired that night. Did we get to the lot and pick out the tree for our dormitory? I assume we did. I don't remember it. We probably had fun hauling it back to campus, setting it up, and decorating it. I can't remember a bit of it. That's not what consumes my memory of that night.

I only recall the sight of the kind, slender man who came to our rescue along a deserted highway. The man who instinctively knew what he needed to do to help us. Who did so without any explanation. Who did it for no monetary reward. Who drove off down the highway leaving five college girls utterly speechless!

Never will I doubt God's attention to my needs. I've experienced His loving and miraculous care. He has gentle messengers to send on His behalf to meet the needs of His children. If no one else is available to help, God will send an angel with just the right equipment. That's exactly what He did for us that night.

The story comes to mind often as a keen reminder of God's attentiveness and of His unerring ability to provide precisely what I need exactly when I need it. I believe He delights in placing me in situations which help me recognize His goodness. The lesson mirrored nothing I'd experienced before or since then. But when a story is this special, once in a lifetime serves as all the evidence needed to be assured that God's presence never fails.

I cannot thank Him enough.

The Rubber and the Road

Lorna Skylar

It was easily the worst day of my life. Divorce. The big D. I never thought it would happen to me. We were happy—or so I thought. We were active church members and parents, with a loving family, close friends . . . and secrets.

I don't think of my ex-husband as a bad man, but at that moment he wanted more. More money, more things, more friends, more life. Just more. All of a sudden I wasn't enough. I had to go.

On the day he moved out, I took our kids out for breakfast. I didn't want them to see their dad moving his things out of our family home, and I wanted to let them know that everything would be OK. They were shattered. I didn't know where we were going to live, or how we were going to make it, but I promised them that it would all be OK. I was lying when I said it, because there was no way I could possibly know that. But I told them that I would never, ever leave them, no matter what. My heart wrenched in my chest when my 17-year-old son, 3 months away from graduating high school, captain of the swim team, captain of the water polo team, honor roll student, looked at me with tears in his eyes and said, "It's OK, Mom. I'll quit school and get a job. I can support us."

I also found out that day that I had $25,000 in credit card debt that I knew nothing about; as time went on, we would have debt collectors calling the house because we were 3 months behind in our payments. The checking account was $500 in the red because my ex had overdrawn it in his relentless pursuit of bigger-better-more. He also told me that he would take all of the cars, not pay any financial support, and keep his retirement account all to himself. That I would have to sell the house. The blows just kept coming. Each one felt as though he had physically struck me. I couldn't breathe or think. I do remember arguing back over these outrageous requests, but he wouldn't give in.

> **Never will I leave you; never will I forsake you.**
>
> —HEBREWS 13:5 (NIV)

I felt like I was walking around in space. Sounds were muffled and echoed in my mind. Everyone was moving in slow motion. Even the poor dog knew something was happening. She cowered and whimpered in the corner. I didn't have the strength to comfort her.

I did hold it together the rest of the day, although I do not know how. My husband removed everything he wanted from our home and left. The kids and I were silent for a long time that afternoon, but we stayed close to one another. We ate dinner. I don't know what. He had hoarded our grocery money for the last 3 weeks in preparation for making his escape, so there was nothing in the house to eat.

Day turned into night, and my mind still raced. *Where will we go? What will we do? How am I going to do this on my own?*

OK, God. This is it. Right here is where the rubber meets the road. Do I really trust You as much as I say I do? Do I truly believe what I say I do?

I cried as I got ready for bed. My head was throbbing. I could barely breathe. I changed clothes and walked toward the bed, knowing I could not sleep a wink with all this turmoil. It was Sunday. We had gone to church in the morning as a happy family. No one knew there was a problem, except me. I bore the weight of this on my frail and weak shoulders, alone.

I had to go to work the next day, and the kids had school. Tears streamed down my face. *God, please,* was all I could get out.

And that's when it happened. My miracle. When I laid my head down on my pillow, it wasn't a pillow. It was a shoulder. And then two strong but gentle arms circled me. They were warm and loving. A sweet, musky scent surrounded me. I inhaled it deeply, wiped away my tears, and drifted off to sleep.

The next morning, I convinced myself I had imagined it. I got myself and the kids ready and we went off to face the day. It was September 11, 2001. On the way to work I listened to the horrifying accounts of planes slamming into the Twin Towers in New York City. *Oh, sweet Jesus! We're at war.*

My father served in Vietnam. I remember that time well. As a child I watched the terrifying stories on the news each night, desperately waiting for news of the war ending so my Dad could come home. And now, I was afraid I would have to send my only son, my firstborn child, off into that same danger. *I can't—Jesus, I can't.*

I struggled all day. I pasted a smile on my face and made my way to my desk, where I tried to hide. I knew if I had to say out loud what had happened, I would completely lose all composure, so I kept it a secret from my coworkers. I lied to them, as I lied to myself, and told them everything was fine. But when night came, I broke down. In the quiet of my bedroom that I once shared with my husband, I knew I was more alone than I had ever been.

Until I laid down on my pillow.

Night after night I crawled into bed, and into the arms of my Savior. My head rested gently on His shoulder, and His warm loving arms held me while I slept. It gave me the strength I needed to face the day. Each day I got a little bit stronger. Each sunrise reminded me that I was not alone.

> **I can do all this through him who gives me strength.**
>
> —PHILIPPIANS 4:13 (NIV)

The fight with my soon-to-be ex-husband was a daily struggle. It was very humbling to be arguing over relatively small things like cars and tools after 25 years and two kids together. But with each new argument, my inner strength and confidence grew. The last major fight we had was two weeks after he'd moved out. It was a barn-burner, but I refused to back down. I was not going to let him walk all over us any longer. I stood my ground with a courage I never knew I had. He stood and stared at me as though he couldn't believe what he was seeing, and then quietly walked away. I thanked Jesus for staying by my side through it all. That night when I lay down, the shoulder and the arms were gone. I smiled. *I'm good now, God. Thank You.*

My son graduated top of his class with honors. He enrolled in college that same fall. We sold the family home and moved across town. This ended up being the best move we could have made. The new neighborhood was much quieter, safer, and far more beautiful. It was closer to work and to all of the amenities that I use regularly. I am still in this home today.

GOD'S GIFT OF TOUCH
— Tez Brooks —

HE TOLD THE persecution story as if it had happened yesterday, though more than a year had passed. He was a stranger to me then, but he has become like a brother since.

The description was graphic. For his beliefs, they had inflicted so much pain on him that he couldn't think about anything else. Except for the most important thing, the Lord in whose service he'd come so far.

"I asked God to please let me die," he said. "But then I saw Jesus and He put his arms around me. They continued to beat me, but the pain was gone."

No more pain, only the warm touch of God.

Thank You, Lord, that You heal the brokenhearted and bind our wounds, as You remind us in Psalm 147:3.

I do not walk through the problems of life alone. My God and Savior are with me always. *I will NEVER leave you or forsake you*, He promised. But it took me being thrust into the loneliest position I have ever been in for me to truly see and feel that promise. I learned that it is one thing to believe something in your head, and another to feel it in your heart.

People in my life may come and go. But God will always be there. He lives in my heart. I feel Him there.

He promised.

And I believe.

Angel with a Business Card

Marilyn Turk

Get children up, fed, and dressed for school. Check.
Get myself dressed. Check.
Throw load of clothes in washer. Check.
Take something out of freezer to thaw for dinner. Check.
Wash breakfast dishes. Check.
Take children to school. Check.
Take dog to vet for surgery. Check.

Now get to my first customer, one of many I had to see that day.

Just a typically hectic day where I had to take care of everything and everyone. I was so busy, yet I felt so alone. Everything seemed to fall on my shoulders. My husband left work early in the morning and didn't come home until late. I took care of the home, the children, and the pets while working a full-time job. Those were the thoughts running endlessly through my mind when...

Bam!! A car ran into the side of mine—the driver's side, not far from where I was sitting—as I was driving through a green light. I watched in shock as our two vehicles moved together in what felt like slow motion, at first stuck side by side as we slid through the intersection, then separating and heading in different directions. The next thing I knew, I was rolling toward a light pole, its concrete base certain to crush the front of the car. It seemed to take endless amounts of time to get there, yet I was powerless to do anything about it. I braced myself mentally for the next collision, but somehow the car stopped before hitting the pole.

What had just happened? A car wreck? *I don't have time for this. I have to get to work.*

Tasting blood, I wondered if I was hurt.

But I couldn't be. I had too much to do. I needed to call my boss or my customer or do something! Too many people depended on me.

> "Come to me, all you who are weary and burdened, and I will give you rest."
>
> —MATTHEW 11:28 (NIV)

I frantically tried to think of what to do, but for some reason, I couldn't move.

Tapping. Someone was tapping on my window. I looked to see who it was, and a man motioned for me to roll the window down. The car was still running, so the power window slid down.

The man asked, "Are you OK?"

In a daze, I said, "I think so." But why was I tasting blood? I lifted my arm to position the visor mirror so I could see myself. There was red on my lip. Apparently, I had bitten through it during the collision.

"But I need to call my boss." I tried to reach the glove compartment for the instructions on what to do in an accident, since I was driving a company car. For some reason, I couldn't reach that far. Turned out, the seat belt wouldn't let me.

The man said, "Don't worry about that. It will be OK. You need to sit here and wait for the ambulance to take you to the hospital. And turn the car off if you can."

"But . . . I need to . . ."

He touched my shoulder and said, "Don't worry about anything. Just relax. Everything will be all right." Then he handed me a business card. "If you need anything, call me."

I took it and nodded. He walked away.

The next time I saw him, he was talking to a policeman, motioning to me. The policeman came over and asked how I was, then told me to stay put until the ambulance arrived. He never questioned me about the accident, so I assumed he knew I was the innocent party.

The ambulance arrived and took me to the hospital. While I was there, I was able to call my boss and tell him what happened, apologizing for not being able to go see my customers that morning. He was sympathetic and understanding, saying he would take care of contacting them. He also told me to make sure I was checked out by the doctors and had no injuries.

Later that day, I was released from the hospital unhurt. I called a neighbor and asked her to please come take me home. Once at home, I called the towing service to track down my car. The company was also a body shop, and the manager asked me how the accident had happened.

After I explained the sequence of events to him, he said, "You were lucky. That other car hit your car right in front of your door. If it had hit your car directly on your door like most T-bone collisions, you might not have survived. Someone must have been looking out for you."

Then he asked, "Were there any other cars in the street?"

I couldn't remember seeing any, despite the fact that it was the intersection of two busy streets.

"I don't know."

"Lucky for you that you didn't run into another car."

Lucky?

I disconnected the phone, mulling over what he said. Then I recalled the feeling of rolling toward the concrete pole that I was certain I was going to hit. But my car stopped. How? What if I had hit the pole and it had collapsed onto my car? I would have been crushed. There were so many "ifs" that didn't happen, including the fact that I wasn't injured. Someone had indeed been looking out for me.

A few days later, I remembered the nice man who had come to my car to calm me down, to give me peace in the middle of the panic. I wanted to thank him and let him know how things turned out. I called the number on the card and asked the receptionist to speak to him. But she said no one by that name worked for their company.

> I am always with you; you hold me by my right hand.
>
> —PSALM 73:23 (NIV)

"Are you sure?" I asked. "I have his card."

"What's the name again?"

I told her and she said, "I've worked here for 10 years, and I'm sure we've never had any employee by that name."

There was no question in my mind that the man had been an angel sent by God to comfort me and give me peace. Above and beyond the accident, He was letting me know that I was not alone, that I didn't have to feel as if I was carrying everyone's burdens on my shoulders. God was watching over me all the time, even when I was too busy to notice.

Who knew angels had business cards?

Angels on the Exit Ramp
Sue McCusker

I stepped out of my car onto the dark highway. It was late at night, and there wasn't even a streetlight in sight. "What am I going to do?" I wondered out loud.

I was on my way home from my Sunday night church group when I heard a *thump* coming from my car, followed by a wobbling noise. I pulled over and discovered I had blown a tire on my car. I had just moved to Atlanta for my first job after college, and I was alone without much money. Although I was unfamiliar with the area, I knew it was not a place I wanted to be stranded in late at night by myself.

These were the days before cell phones, so I had no choice but to leave my car. There was just one problem: I knew there were no gas stations or anything else nearby at this exit. There was no point in going back to my broken-down car, but I didn't know how far I would have to walk to get help.

I didn't even have a flashlight with me. I stomped through the tall grass on the side of the road and headed toward the exit ramp just ahead. The road was isolated and dark, and no other cars were in sight. I tried to stay hidden in the tall grass from anyone who might come by.

Afraid, I began to pray. *Please, Lord, keep me from harm until I can get to a place of safety.*

At that very moment, the headlights of an approaching car appeared behind me, driving slowly up the exit ramp from the highway until the car was right next to me. What did they want, and how could they see me so easily? I kept my head down and continued walking in the tall grass, hoping the car would pass without stopping. But it was useless. The car came to a halt near me, and the window on the passenger side rolled down. I didn't know who to expect, but I was quite surprised to see an older woman with gray hair and kind-looking eyes lean her head out the window.

"I see you're having car trouble," the woman said with a smile.

> God is our refuge and strength, an ever-present help in trouble.
>
> —PSALM 46:1 (NIV)

I wanted to deny it and go on my way, but they would have already passed my car, and there was no other reason for me to be walking out here this late at night. "Yes." I tried to sound confident. "But I'm just walking up to the top of the exit ramp to go to the gas station for help." I hoped she would not see through my bluff and realize that there was no gas station in sight.

"Nonsense," she quickly replied, not even looking around to confirm my story. "Get in. You can use our car phone."

Car phones at the time were a luxury that only a few people were lucky enough to have. They were expensive and could only be used while plugged into the car. I wasn't sure about this, so I peered into the passenger window to see who was driving. It was another older woman, also with gray hair and a friendly smile. Both women were very well dressed, wearing lots of beautiful jewelry and driving a big, luxurious Cadillac. *Well,* I thought, *they certainly look harmless.* But what were a couple of older, well-dressed women doing out this late?

"That's OK," I replied politely. "It's a short walk from here; I don't mind." It was not like me to get into a stranger's car late at night.

"Nonsense," the woman said again, smiling. She sat there, waiting. "We're on our way home. We have time."

Considering my situation, it seemed like my best and only option, despite my worry. They didn't look like they needed to rob me, and two older women didn't seem like much of a threat. *If I were them,* I thought, *I'd be more afraid of me robbing them, but they don't seem afraid at all.*

"OK." I cautiously climbed into their Cadillac's back seat, and they handed me their car phone.

I managed to call a wrecker service and hung up, then thanked the ladies for the use of their phone. "I'll go wait in my car now, and you can go on your way."

"No, we'll wait," the woman who had been doing all the speaking insisted. "You stay here." They were in no hurry to leave.

It was close to midnight now, and no other cars had come by. I settled into the back seat and tried not to fidget. The two women didn't say much while we waited. From the back seat, I saw only the back of their heads, because they looked straight ahead the entire time—their eyes focused out the windshield into the darkness ahead as if they were watching or guarding something.

They didn't ask me anything. There were none of the usual questions someone might ask a stranger sitting in the back seat of their car. None of the typical conversations like your name, where you live, or what you do for a living. Not once did they look back over their shoulder or glance in the rearview mirror as people tend to do when there's someone sitting behind them. Occasionally, I would hear them talk to each other, but their voices were too low for me to understand what they were saying. Like chauffeurs, they seemed to be "on the job."

Finally, I saw the wrecker pull up behind my car, which was off to the side of the road at the bottom of the exit ramp. I thanked the two women again and said I'd go work with the mechanic now, and they could go home.

"No, we'll wait," the woman replied again. Neither of them moved from their position in the front seat.

I got out of the Cadillac and walked back to my car. I watched as the mechanic changed my tire in the dark. After he finished, I started my car again to make sure everything was OK, and it wouldn't start! The car chugged, but wouldn't turn over. My car battery had died. *What else could happen?* I thought. I waited longer as the mechanic hooked up the jumper cables to start my battery. I glanced up ahead; the Cadillac was still waiting in the dark.

After about an hour, everything was finally fixed. I settled the bill with the mechanic and wrote him a check.

"Who is that in the car up ahead?" the mechanic asked as he took the check from my hand.

"Oh, they're waiting for me," I tried to say casually.

"Hmm," the man huffed.

> **The name of the LORD is a strong tower; the righteous run to it and are safe.**
>
> —PROVERBS 18:10 (NKJV)

I returned to my car and let out a sigh of relief when the engine turned over. As I pulled onto the exit ramp, I wanted to wave goodbye to the two women who had patiently waited with me all this time, but I didn't have a chance. As soon as I began to move, they also pulled out in front of me, matching my movement. They drove on ahead of me and soon disappeared into the night. I didn't see where their car went after that as I headed home.

Later that night, when I was safely back in my apartment, I thought about the events and wished I'd had a chance to thank the two older women one more time for helping me. As I sat on the side of my bed and thanked God for answering my prayer and keeping me safe, I somehow felt that the two women were aware of it as well. The angels on the exit ramp had looked out for me and made me feel safe, just like I had asked my heavenly Father to do.

God's Heavenly Messenger
Sara Etgen-Baker

One day while I was out walking, I caught my foot on a crack in the sidewalk and plunged to the ground. I tried to break my fall using my right arm, but still landed hard on the concrete, and immediately heard an audible pop. Pain shot through my right shoulder and down my upper right arm. The following morning, my arm was so unbelievably weak that I couldn't lift it. The pain in my right shoulder was so intense that it was like I was walking around with a knife in it. I didn't go to the doctor, however, assuming I'd get better over time. I accepted my condition and carried on as normally as possible, frequently using my left arm instead of my right, administering analgesic creams to my upper right arm and shoulder and taking over-the-counter pain relievers. But the pain and weakness intensified, eventually disturbing my sleep.

After 4 months, I finally admitted to myself that I wasn't improving and sought the advice of an orthopedic specialist.

"The symptoms you're describing sound like a torn rotator cuff," Dr. Dodson suggested.

"Are you sure?" I asked, disbelief creeping into my voice.

"The only way I'll know for sure is with an MRI of your shoulder. Here," she said, handing me some paperwork, "take this order to the imaging facility across the street. You can have your MRI done today."

"Today?"

"Yes, today. No need to wait. Come back tomorrow, and I'll discuss the results with you."

I returned to Dr. Dodson's office the next day; together we looked at the scan. "You see this tear here," she said, pointing to a rather lengthy tear on my rotator cuff. "You can either have surgery immediately to repair it or wait and have a cortisone shot in your shoulder to reduce the pain and give the tear time to heal. However, I have to advise you that it's highly unlikely it will heal on its own."

My fear of surgery took hold, and I quickly chose the second option. Within a week after receiving the cortisone shot, my pain diminished significantly, convincing me that I was healing. However, six weeks later the pain returned with a vengeance.

"You'll need to see my colleague, Dr. Markman, an orthopedic surgeon," Dr. Dodson advised when I consulted her over the phone. "The sooner the better."

The following day I found myself sitting next to Dr. Markman as he reviewed the MRI. I watched his eyes, alert for any slight change in his facial expression and demeanor, dreading the inevitable.

"You need rotator cuff surgery," he said candidly. "I'll schedule your surgery for next month. The hospital will be in touch with details." He left the exam room before I could ask the sudden rush of questions racing through my mind.

His assistant measured my arm for the post-surgery sling and shoulder immobilizer. "The hospital and the anesthesiologist will reach out to you a week before surgery." He escorted me out of the exam room. "You may message me through the patient portal with any questions you may have," he said, handing me his business card with the portal information on the back.

Questions? Of course, I had questions—gazillions of them. Since I'd never had surgery, I spent the weeks before surgery incessantly worrying, questions mounting in my mind: What will surgery be like? Will my throat hurt after the anesthesiologist removes the breathing tube? How will I react to anesthesia? Will I be nauseous after surgery? How can I possibly sleep in that sling? How will I cope with long-term pain and being dependent upon my husband 24/7 for 6 weeks? Are we up for this challenge?

> **Last night an angel of the God to whom I belong and whom I serve stood beside me.**
>
> —ACTS 27:23 (NIV)

All of those questions and more swirled around in my head, keeping me awake at night. When I slept, I had a lot of vivid dreams. In one such dream, I saw a trapped bird and heard it frantically flapping its wings in a panic. That's the way I felt—trapped, helpless, and afraid. I became increasingly restless, agitated, anxious, and terrified. I neglected prayer; I forgot about seeking God's guidance and reassurance. Instead, I consulted a psychiatrist, quickly becoming dependent upon the anxiety medication and sleep aid she prescribed.

The days and weeks passed painfully slowly until the surgery date finally arrived. All I remember of that day is being driven to the hospital, putting on a hospital gown, lying down on a gurney, and being wheeled to the operating room. I woke up hours later, nausea-free, without any recollection of the actual operating room, the anesthesia, or the surgery. As promised, my bandaged right arm was in a sling with a thick, cumbersome, restrictive shoulder immobilizer.

Once home, I was helpless, incapable of using my right arm and hand for even the basics like eating, brushing my teeth, showering, dressing myself, and so forth. Sleep eluded me. Silent grenades of pain were my constant companion. I thought I'd feel as if there were knives in my shoulder and arm forever. Some days it felt as if I were making an effort of will just to exist, with no emotional energy left over to read the Bible or the other books on my nightstand. Every day was a battle between losing hope and having faith in healing and physical therapy.

One pain-filled night, I remembered the power of prayer and began praying, asking God to ease my physical and emotional suffering and help my shoulder heal: "God, I've ignored prayer, and I haven't sought You in my time of need. I come to You now asking for Your forgiveness and mercy. My body is weak and in pain from the surgery. Grant my body more strength, relieve it of this pain, help it heal, and ease my suffering."

There was no immediate answer. But another night, not too long after that, I awoke with the sense of someone sitting beside me, holding my hand and comforting me. I looked around, but no one was there—not even my husband.

I fell back to sleep but quickly awakened, this time to the sensation of someone rubbing my right shoulder, stroking my hair, and gently hugging me.

I sat up and looked around. No one was physically there, but the feeling that someone or something was there was real, powerful, and calming. Although I'd long believed angels existed, I had never actually encountered one—not until that night. I eased back to sleep, remembering Billy Graham's words: "Believers, look up—take courage. The angels are nearer than you think."

For weeks, I frequently awakened to the same loving touch, reassuring embrace, and relief from pain. The warmth, encouragement, and love I received came from what I believe was one of God's angels sent to comfort me. Many nights it was by my side as I recovered and healed, transforming and strengthening me and giving me the courage to alleviate my dependence on pain medications.

I've long since recovered from my surgery, but I vividly remember my encounter with God and His heavenly messenger who visited with me and helped me. He and his angel are with me still, especially when I'm concerned or troubled. I awaken during those restless nights taking solace in God's presence and His heavenly messenger with its angelic, comforting touch and warm embrace.

> **See, I am sending an angel ahead of you to guard you along the way and to bring you to the place I have prepared.**
>
> —EXODUS 23:20 (NIV)

The golden moments in the stream of life rush past us, and we see nothing but sand; the angels come to visit, and we only know them when they are gone.

—George Eliot

CHAPTER 2
Mysterious Strangers

Help at Just the Right Time 54
    Karen Register, as told to Laura Bailey

Angel at the Train Station 58
    Margaret McNeil

An Unexpected Answer to Prayer 63
    Laurie Jeron

The Nurse in the Hospital Ward 68
    Rachel Britton

Prince of Peace. 73
    Elizabeth Brown

Miracle in Frankfurt 77
    Sharon Beth Brani

God Showed Up. 83
    Patricia Cameron

Help at Just the Right Time

Karen Register, as told to Laura Bailey

I walked around the house, filled with nervous energy, waiting for my granddaughters to arrive. I was excited to have them visit me for a week while my daughter went on a work trip. The cabinets were filled with juice boxes, sweet treats, and snack packs, ready to grab and take with us on the many outings I had planned. I couldn't help but laugh as I added more pillows to the guest bed, knowing my oldest granddaughter would be spending her nights snuggled with me.

As keen as I was to see them—since they lived almost 8 hours away, we didn't have the opportunity to visit often—I was a bit anxious, too. This was the first time I would have both granddaughters simultaneously, and many years had passed since I'd navigated days with a baby and toddler. Still, when my daughter asked if I could watch the girls while she traveled for business, I jumped at the opportunity.

"Nona! Where are you?" My sweet three-year-old granddaughter, Madeline, stood at the front door, banging her little fists, her face barely visible in the door's glass. I could scarcely unlock the door before she grasped me in a big bear hug; grinning, she whispered, "I am so glad I'm here. Did you know Mommy is going away, and it will just be us?" My heart melted, but almost immediately the worry began again. *It's only a week,* I told myself. *It will be OK; I can do this!*

After putting the girls to bed that night, I told my husband I was thinking of taking them shopping tomorrow. I wanted to take both girls out briefly before taking on a bigger adventure later in the week. My husband offered to go with me, but I assured him I would be OK. I felt comfortable navigating the car seats, and we would just go to one store and come home. "We shouldn't be gone for more than an hour."

> **Look to the LORD and his strength; seek his face always.**
>
> —1 CHRONICLES 16:11 (NIV)

At breakfast the following day, I told Madeline that we would go shopping after we ate and cleaned up. I told her to grab her pocketbook and put 2 dollars in her change purse because I would allow her to purchase two items at the store. Excited, her face lit up, and she ran to tell her grandfather about her upcoming plans. As Madeline talked with my husband and the baby napped, I went to my room to get ready.

Before I hopped in the shower, I took a few minutes to pray and ask the Lord to calm my spirit and give me strength. I prayed for our safety traveling to and from the store and for an overall uneventful trip. As I finished getting ready, I felt a sense of peace, and chastised myself for being so worried. It was a simple trip to the store. What could go wrong?

As we turned into the parking lot, I thanked the Lord for the abundance of empty spaces and lack of crowds and navigated the car into a spot close to the door. I wrestled the car seats, choosing to leave the heavy diaper bag in the car. We would be in and out in less than 10 minutes, easy peasy.

I positioned the baby on my hip and grabbed Madeline's hand. "OK, Madeline, this is important. Listen to Nona. We are about to enter the store, but there are cars driving around the parking lot. Please make sure to hold my hand at all times, and once we get into the store, stay with me." Her dimples appeared as her lips began to turn upward in a big smile, and she nodded in agreement. I squeezed her hand, and we headed for the store's entrance.

The next thing I knew, I was on my back. To this day I don't remember exactly what happened; there was nothing in the parking lot that might have made me trip, and I'm not prone to dizzy spells. I didn't have time to think about it, because once I realized I was on the ground the first thing I noticed was that the baby's head was centimeters from the pavement. I was so confused. *What just happened? Where is Madeline?*

Then I saw my granddaughter standing alone in the middle of the lane between the parking lot and the store. Unable to control my panic, fearful she would be hit by a passing car, I called out to her to quickly walk to the sidewalk. My hands shook nervously, as I was trying to keep an eye on Madeline and examine the baby to make sure she wasn't hurt.

Once I'd assured myself that the baby was all right, I looked up to find a woman standing over me. She helped me to my feet, and I saw another woman walk Madeline over to me. The women had appeared out of nowhere; I hadn't seen them before I fell. At the time, I didn't think much about it. I was bleeding badly from a scrape that went from my wrist to my elbow, and it felt like I'd sprained my ankle. Shakily, I checked over the baby again and started hobbling toward

Madeline. The two ladies helped us enter the store, placing both girls in a cart.

I turned around to thank them, and they were gone! I searched the entire store, going back outside to see if they were heading back to their cars or walking into another shop, but there was no one.

Later, recalling the day's events with my husband, I couldn't stop wondering where the women had come from. The parking lot had been empty; I was one of the only cars parked near the store's entrance. It couldn't have been more than a few seconds from when we started walking to the curb and my fall. It would have been impossible for someone who wasn't nearby to come to my aid so quickly. And where did they go once we were in the store? It wasn't a big shop, and I know I didn't see them walk out the doors; how did they just disappear?

To this day I have no answer to those questions. All I can say is that I think the Lord answered my prayer for strength and safety by sending angels to help me and protect my grandbabies.

> But you, LORD, do not be far from me. You are my strength; come quickly to help me.
>
> —PSALM 22:19 (NIV)

I was shaken by the incident, and for a few days afterward I had to ice my ankle and my wrist, but I was aware that the day could have ended very differently. The baby could have been significantly injured, Madeline could have been hurt, or I could have had something much worse than a sprained ankle. God was there, watching over me and my granddaughters, protecting them from lasting harm, and sending angels at just the right time.

Angel at the Train Station
Margaret McNeil

The train station was bustling. People grabbed a quick bite to eat in the food court, bought miscellaneous sundries in stores scattered around the station, and rushed to catch trains. I heard numerous languages spoken around me. Some I recognized, while others were unfamiliar, but I didn't hear the only language I knew—English.

Less than two weeks earlier, my husband, son, and I flew from our home in Memphis to visit our youngest son in Germany. Due to work obligations, my husband could only stay 10 days. The morning he flew home from Berlin, my sons and I boarded a train bound for Vienna to spend some time touring the city.

To save time and money, we chose a route that required us to change trains in Prague. Although the Czech Republic was no longer the communist country I had learned about in school, I was especially nervous about this leg of the trip. What would I do if my sons and I got separated? Would anyone speak English? Would I be able to find the platform for our next train? Before our trip, I shared my fear with close friends, siblings, and God.

My anxiety increased with each passing mile. By the time we disembarked, I wondered if my nervousness was obvious to my fellow travelers. As people whizzed past us, I searched for a kiosk where I could exchange a euro note for korunas, the Czech currency. Once this obstacle was out of the way, we went in search of somewhere to eat lunch.

Our layover was only 90 minutes long, so we decided to split up. My sons took the korunas and stood in a very long line at a fast-food restaurant, leaving me to find a table. After walking around the lively food court a couple of times, I finally spotted an empty table with four chairs. I sat down, relieved that I had not only found a table, but also that my sons were within eyeshot. As I watched all the activity around me, I felt like the proverbial fish out of water.

I was barely situated when an elderly gentleman with a cane approached my table. He was sharply dressed, wearing a button-down shirt, brown pants, brown plaid jacket, and a hat. He had piercing brown eyes, sun-kissed skin, and furrowed brow. He spoke to me in an unfamiliar language.

> **Do not forget to show hospitality to strangers, for by so doing some people have shown hospitality to angels without knowing it.**
>
> —HEBREWS 13:2 (NIV)

"*Sprechen Sie Englisch?*" I asked in faltering German.

He smiled and shook his head no. He pointed to one of the chairs. I held up three fingers to let him know we didn't need the fourth chair. I assumed he was going to take it to another table, but he didn't. He pulled out the chair and sat down across from me. His warm and inviting brown eyes lit up every time he smiled, which was quite often. He was a calming presence in a stressful place, and I felt my anxiety melting away. I wished that I could converse with this kind soul. For 15 minutes, we exchanged awkward smiles—strangers from different continents—without saying a word, the silence broken only by the noise in the train station.

Mere seconds before my sons arrived with lunch, he stood up, smiled, said something to me, and walked away. He wasn't even out of eyesight when my sons put our food on the table.

I quickly told them what happened and tried to point out the man, but by that time he had disappeared among the throng of travelers.

> **Are not all angels ministering spirits sent to serve those who will inherit salvation?**
>
> — HEBREWS 1:14 (NIV)

When we finished eating, we went in search of the electronic departure board to find the platform for the train to Vienna. After we found it, I spotted the elderly gentleman standing with two other men and discreetly pointed him out to my sons. When he saw me, a huge smile spread across his face as he left his companions and quickly walked over to us.

"The train listing to Vienna will be posted shortly," he said in English. There were dozens of trains listed on the board, so I asked him how he knew we were going to Vienna.

"I didn't," he replied. "I'm an assistant who helps give directions." He smiled, turned around, and once again disappeared into the crowd.

I was shocked he spoke English and astounded he knew where we were going. After all, he and I never spoke at the table and none of our luggage had information on it showing our destination. I didn't have time to ponder what took place

GOD'S GIFT OF HEARING
— Kimberly Shumate —

IN LUKE 11:28 (NIV), Jesus says, "Blessed rather are those who hear the word of God and obey it." Hearing God's voice isn't always an easy thing. He speaks through His Word and the Holy Spirit, yet fails to get our attention. He'll use someone or something to gain our interest, to no avail. As a last resort, He will allow a difficult circumstance—a thorn in the flesh, fear, confusion, or anxiety that slows us to a crawl then a stop. It's there, at the end of ourselves, that God can finally be heard—in the silence of desperation. He is close now. Listen . . .

---

because moments later—just like he said—the Vienna platform information was posted.

Shortly after boarding and finding our seats, the train pulled out of Prague. I talked to my sons about what had just happened.

"I thought you said he didn't speak English," exclaimed my oldest son.

"He implied he didn't," I responded. "How did he know we were going to Vienna?"

"You probably said something without realizing it," said my youngest son. My sons brushed off the encounter as if nothing out of the ordinary had happened and thought I was making much ado about nothing.

As the train weaved its way across the Czech countryside, I couldn't stop thinking about this man. He showed up when

I was feeling the most anxious about this trip. I felt a tremendous sense of peace while he sat with me that disappeared when he did. He knew where we were headed. I replayed the events over and over in my mind and realized our meeting was not just a coincidence.

When I was growing up, my mother told me of times in her life when an "angel unaware" showed up to help her with a predicament. These angelic helpers didn't have wings or halos. Instead, they had an uncanny ability to show up out of nowhere, at just the right time and place, and give assistance. When their work was done, they'd disappear as quickly as they arrived. I always wondered if this would ever happen to me, and if I would recognize it if it did.

By the time the train pulled into the station in Vienna four-and-a-half hours later, I knew I'd encountered my own angel unaware. Not only had I recognized it, but my sons were able to share the experience with me. Maybe one day, they'll tell their children about their mother's encounter with an angel at the train station.

An Unexpected Answer to Prayer

Laurie Jeron

It was a beautiful late spring week, sunny with mild temperatures and no humidity. Yet a storm of apprehension and anxiety was brewing inside of me and my mom as we wondered what would happen on Saturday.

The story begins years earlier as we returned from a family vacation. We pulled into the driveway to find the signpost advertising our business, a music school, lying almost flat on the ground of our front lawn. The best we could determine was that a truck had backed into it, pushing it over. My dad got out of the car and, like Superman, pulled the post up with his bare hands. The pipe was sliced open, but it was upright, and when we flipped the light switch on it still worked. Dad used some black electrical tape to cover the gaping hole so that no one would get hurt on the jagged metal. It had remained usable for decades, holding up through heavy rain, gusty winds, hurricanes, and snowstorms.

Now, though, the post was showing signs of weakness. Almost daily we had to straighten it as it drooped and leaned. We could no longer deny that it needed replacing.

My dad was approaching his golden years. His function had declined significantly in the previous year. He would often mention how his strength was less than half of what it had been the year before, and he could no longer do the things he once did. His Superman days had passed.

Still, he insisted on fixing the post himself, and his declining strength was only part of the reason Mom and I were worried. Dad also had a short fuse, and when things didn't go well, his temper would flare. You didn't want to be around when he blew.

> **Come quickly to help me, my LORD and my Savior.**
>
> —PSALM 38:22 (NIV)

To make matters worse from my perspective, no one was available to help him that weekend. Not my brother, my uncles, or family friends. That meant he would want my mom to help him. She was always faithfully by his side, working along with him.

I remember them removing wallpaper, taking down walls, and even pouring sidewalk blocks and curbs. My mom is strong and fierce, as were the women who came before her. They taught me well, providing living examples of the "wife of noble character" from Proverbs 31 (NIV). Mom wasn't afraid to get dirt under her fingernails, but she wasn't a young woman anymore, and I was worried about both of them.

As Saturday edged closer, my anxiety levels climbed higher. I prayed for peace and calm, but I was still waiting for peace to arrive as Saturday morning dawned. It was a picture-perfect day. The neighborhood was bustling with people out walking. Families, friends, baby carriages, and dogs strolled down the street. The sound of lawn mowers and leaf blowers filled the air and the aroma of freshly cut grass permeated the atmosphere. Our next-door neighbors were planting flower beds. Kids were out playing, their laughter filling the air. Meanwhile, Dad was getting ready to start working.

I sat at my desk, praying, "Please help him, Lord. May it go smoothly and without any issues. Keep him calm, and don't let his temper flare. Give Mom extra grace and strength. Increase Dad's strength for the task at hand. In Jesus's name, amen."

Dad turned off the electricity first. The old post would be removed next. Would he be strong enough to loosen the bolts holding the post in place? And the next step was where things could go awry. The new post would need to be installed, and the likelihood that the bolts would be in the exact same spot as they were in the current post were slim to none. New holes would have to be drilled into the cement-and-brick foundation that the post stood upon, and I knew my dad didn't have the correct tools for the job. To say I was concerned was an understatement. This was a recipe for a *Titanic*-level disaster: it could go down quickly.

I checked on them several times, bringing cold drinks. Mom was at Dad's side helping, as always. I offered to join in, but they said they were OK. I headed back inside to resume my work.

Then the unexpected occurred. My mom ran into the house and exclaimed, "You'll never guess what just happened!" She described how a man who lived in the condominiums across the street walked over and asked Dad what he was doing. The neighbor offered to give him a hand loosening the bolts. As they talked, he said he had the tool that Dad needed to drill into the concrete and would loan it to him. A few minutes later, he returned with the tool in hand. He and his wife were on their way out, he told them, but he drilled the first hole and helped Dad mark the other three before leaving. He said he would come over when they got home and see if he could help finish it up.

He had struck up a conversation with my mom, too, commenting about our music school. "I see you give drum lessons.

My grandson loves the drums. He always takes pots and containers, spatulas, spoons—whatever he can get his hands on—and he drums on everything."

"He might like lessons," Mom had responded. Then she asked how old the neighbor's grandson was.

"Three."

"That's a little young. We don't usually start kids on lessons until they're five or six. But my daughter played the drums in high school, and she's very patient with young students. I'll ask her about giving your grandson a few trial lessons."

He said he was thrilled to hear that and headed off with his wife to their family party.

The rest of the day went perfectly. It couldn't have been better. It was all quiet on the western front—or perhaps it was the southwestern lawn—but I was holding my breath until my parents had finished the job. Finally, the installation was complete, the electricity was turned back on, and everything was working great.

Our neighbor returned later that afternoon and was excited to see the great job Dad had done. Mom and Dad thanked him for loaning us the drill. Mom told him she had spoken to me and we would set up some lessons for his grandson. He thanked her and said they would call me on Monday to set up an appointment.

The following week came and went, but the neighbor never called. I asked my mom if the man had given her a phone

> **Praise the LORD, you his angels, you mighty ones who do his bidding, who obey his word.**
>
> —PSALM 103:20 (NIV)

number, but he hadn't. I was willing to go over to the condos to talk in person, but Mom didn't know which one he lived in. She gave me a general description, but I didn't recall ever seeing anyone in the neighborhood it would fit. Had Mom met the wife? What did she look like? Mom said she never saw her.

Then I asked, "What was his name?"

"He was Latino. His name was Jesus."

You could have knocked me over with a feather at that moment. Could it be? Could my prayer have resulted in a visit from heaven? Was it an angel? Could it have been Jesus Himself? There was no way to know. The neighbor had disappeared without a trace.

Ever since that day, Mom and I have discussed it, and we often smile and wonder. Why did the mysterious Jesus ask about music lessons for his grandchild if he wasn't an ordinary person? We thought it might be so that we would follow up and ask about him—and through those questions, realize that God was watching over us.

Someday we will know for sure. In the meantime, I often remember that day fondly, with a smile on my face and a song of thanksgiving in my heart to the Lord for answered prayers and for lighting the way.

The Nurse in the Hospital Ward
Rachel Britton

You know that moment in a movie where you are about to find out whether the doctor is bringing good news or bad news to the main characters? The director usually gives viewers a clue by having the doctor stop outside the door and pause before entering. That means bad news. After all, a life-threatening diagnosis is bleak and frightening information to share.

But this wasn't a movie. It was my life, and I was the one waiting in a hospital room in the children's ward with my husband, 2-year-old daughter, and 7-week-old twin boys. I was the one who could see the doctor through the glass window of the door, hesitating before entering. And I knew what that meant. Bad news.

The morning had started with both babies fussing and feverish. My friend from England, a NICU (Newborn Intensive Care Unit) nurse, had come to visit and see them. "Call the pediatrician," she told me in a firm but calm voice, "and tell the doctor they have fevers and a rash." I had no idea why this was so important.

The pediatrician examined the boys and then left. The minutes ticked by as we waited in the exam room. Eventually, she returned. "I've spoken to all my colleagues," she said. "We're split 50/50 on whether your babies have meningitis. I am sending you to the local hospital."

And so, that is where we were, waiting for the results from the babies' spinal taps.

The doctor finally entered and told us the bad news. My 7-week-old twin boys, who had each weighed 5 pounds, 10 ounces, at birth and now weighed little more than a newborn at full-term, had bacterial meningitis.

Bacterial meningitis is a serious infection and inflammation of the brain. It can cause permanent damage, such as hearing loss and brain damage, and in some cases it can be fatal.

Immediately the nursing staff flew into action. A large quarantine sign was slapped outside the hospital room door. Each staff member quickly donned gowns and masks. Nurses bent over each baby as they concentrated on inserting IVs into their tiny veins to start administering antibiotics and painkillers. For one of my sons, the IV was inserted into a vein on his head. Tape held the IV, nearly as big as his head, in place.

The small regional hospital could not adequately care for such a high-risk illness. Teams of doctors and nurses from Massachusetts General Hospital in Boston were already preparing for our arrival.

There was no room for myself or my husband in either ambulance. We followed in our car while my friend took our 2-year old daughter, who had no symptoms, home for the night.

As I looked across the Boston skyline, I cried to my husband, "I want to go home." I didn't mean our small suburban house in the nearby town, but the home where we had been born, across the Atlantic in England. We had been living in the States for just over two years. With such a frightening turn of events and not knowing what lay ahead, I wanted the comfort and warmth that physical nearness of family and friends brings when we are in trouble. Of course, that was impossible in our current circumstances, but still I wanted bodily assurance.

We had made friends since coming to the States—people like ourselves with young children, some of whom had also moved from their home country for work. After finding a church to call home, we had started to get established in a church community.

However, a dangerous infection such as bacterial meningitis, which can be passed from person to person, meant that we were isolated, apart from necessary medical staff. Our friends, out of concern for themselves and their families, quite sensibly watched and waited from a distance.

By the time we arrived at MGH in Boston, the babies had been moved onto a ward. They lay close together in one cot, their heads arched back in the abnormal body position that is typical of meningitis. The swelling of the lining of the brain causes a severe headache. Monitors beeped. IVs dripped. Medical staff stood around the bed. The staff seemed barely aware we had entered the room.

> Even though I walk through the darkest valley, I will fear no evil, for you are with me.
>
> —PSALM 23:4 (NIV)

"Will they be OK?" my husband inquired of the doctor. His answer, even though I could only see his back clothed in his white coat, still haunts me. "Let's get through the next twenty-four hours," he answered.

It's natural for a mother to want to comfort her children when they are in distress. Yet, I could do nothing to stop my babies' crying, or settle them. I rocked them and held them close in the hope my familiar heartbeat would soothe them. I tried to nurse them, but they turned their heads away and continued to whimper.

I had run out of ways in which to calm my two precious babies. Having barely recovered my physical strength from the emergency C-section just a few weeks earlier, now my mental strength drained from me as I looked at their tiny, contorted bodies.

And then *she* entered the room. Her broad shoulders filled the space on the other side of the cot. She focused her eyes on the babies as she stooped over, knowing exactly what was needed.

Without a word, she began to work quickly and quietly. Her large hands swiftly and deftly shaped two blankets into ovals like little nests. Then she tenderly and carefully scooped up each baby and nestled him in the middle of a nest. It was as if each were cocooned in the womb. She placed one hand on each baby's tiny body. Within seconds, although I'm sure in reality it was longer, their bodies relaxed. With their heads still strained back, they slept. Peace at last.

With each hand still in place over the babies, she lifted her head. Then she smiled. That beaming face brought instant light into a room that had been dark and heavy with sickness and despair.

Twenty-four hours later, our baby boys were still breathing. The doctors began to hope for a better outcome. Each day they carefully monitored their health and prepared us for the possible outcomes that could lie ahead, including mental disabilities and hearing loss.

Two weeks into our stay, through the diligent investigation of an infectious diseases doctor, the diagnosis was changed from bacterial meningitis to viral meningitis. Unknown to me, the sores that I'd noticed previously in my mouth and on my hands were from Hand, Foot, and Mouth Disease—Coxsackievirus—probably contracted through my daughter at preschool. I had ignored them, because I thought I was just run down from the birth. The babies tested positive for the virus. Unable to fight the virus with their small, vulnerable bodies, it had developed into meningitis.

IVs were removed. Monitors stopped. We were sent home and told to expect a full recovery. Walking through the door into our little house never felt so good.

> **Therefore, as God's chosen people, holy and dearly loved, clothe yourselves with compassion, kindness, humility, gentleness and patience.**
>
> —COLOSSIANS 3:12 (NIV)

My twin boys are now 6-foot-tall, handsome, strapping young men in full health.

I often think about our nurse. She cared for our babies during those darkest moments. And then she disappeared. We never saw her again. I never found out her name. Perhaps she told me, and in the distress of that time I didn't take it in. Yet, I don't even remember having a conversation with her. Just her presence in our hospital room brought overwhelming comfort and a knowledge of God's loving care. I still cherish the tender concern she showed and the solace she brought. I still have a photo of her standing on the other side of the cot, smiling broadly with one hand resting on each of my babies' sickly bodies. I didn't take photos of any of the other nurses or doctors, but I did ask *this* nurse if I could snap a memory of her.

Perhaps one day I will meet her again, or find out who she is. But for me, on a day when fear closed in and I didn't know what to do, I will always remember her as an angel.

Prince of Peace
Elizabeth Brown

In 1979, I was 20 years old and returning to the United States from Japan after a year of college study abroad. On the way home, I planned to visit Taiwan for two days, hoping to visit the National Palace Museum. I'd studied Asian art and wanted to see the collection from mainland China, saved from the purges of the Cultural Revolution. A friend of a friend knew a flight attendant there, and she said I could stay with her family and they would show me around.

When I arrived in Taiwan, the customs agent at the airport flagged me, apparently finding it suspicious that a young female was traveling alone. He wondered why I was in the country for such a short time. "Are you carrying drugs?"

"No," I answered, shocked and suddenly worried that this man was about to cause some serious trouble for me.

I don't even remember praying—I had only recently given my life to Jesus, and I was new to this life of faith—but there was an appeal rising from deep within me, something like *help*. I watched him open my suitcase and throw my belongings, one by one, onto the concrete floor.

I don't remember exactly when it started, but I began to experience a growing sense of peace, like a warmth, rising in my inner being as if I were being swaddled from the inside out. The peace unfurled and blossomed. Although intellectually I knew that being accused of drug smuggling in a foreign country was incredibly dangerous, and that the fact that I was innocent wouldn't necessarily save me, I found myself incapable of worry. No trace of fear was left. The peace had swallowed it up. It was as if I were inside a great cloud suffused with sunlight, and all of it covered me, filling me, protecting me.

> **Peace I leave with you; my peace I give to you. I do not give to you as the world gives. Do not let your hearts be troubled and do not be afraid.**
>
> —JOHN 14:27 (NIV)

The man continued to rummage through my toiletries, clothes, and books. Curious passengers and airport employees turned to see what was happening. Suddenly the man yelled, "Aha!" He held up a rectangular plastic box. The box opened from the top, but also had, on the bottom, what looked like a secret compartment. The man raised it high. He smiled at the crowd gathered around us. Then he looked at me, triumphant. "So. What's in *here* then?"

"Watercolors." My voice was barely audible.

He opened the top to find squares of multicolored paint. Then he ripped off the cover of the "secret compartment" with a flourish. Another dozen watercolor squares tumbled to the floor. Disgusted, he threw the empty box on top of my other belongings, shoved my suitcase toward me and yelled, "Go!"

As I kneeled on the floor, piling my things back into my suitcase, I marveled that I wasn't afraid. There was no room to feel anything but peace. God had protected me—but He wasn't done yet.

The sense of well-being was still with me as I exited the airport and found, to my dismay, there were no taxis. The only way to get to the city, which was almost an hour away, was by bus. Over a dozen buses were lined up, each headed to a different city location. I was supposed to meet the flight attendant at the YMCA. How would I know which bus was the right one? I couldn't read Chinese.

A slow drizzle began to fall. Yet instead of the panic that I might have been feeling before, the peace still held me. I felt carried, as if through air, as I walked to a random line and stood in it. A young man with a large backpack stepped in beside me. "Hello," he said in English, and we struck up a conversation. I learned that he was traveling from New Zealand and knew one of my classmates from Japan. We laughed in amazement. *What are the chances of that?*

I told him of my dilemma. "I know how to get to the YMCA," he said. "I can take you there." True to his word, he guided me to the correct bus.

Time passed quickly as the bus rumbled by tiled-roof houses, tall outbuildings, and rice fields the color of jade. It was early summer, and the hills and trees glowed green. When we finally arrived in the city, the young man—I never learned his name—felt like an old friend. We disembarked, funneled onto city streets filled with more motorbikes than cars. Traversing several city blocks, we crossed crowded intersections and descended into two dimly lit underground tunnels guarded by Taiwanese soldiers with machine guns. Tensions with China were at an all-time high in those days; in 1979, Taiwan was on red alert. I only learned about that later. At the time, I was not afraid. The peace that had been with me in the airport was with me still—almost as if it had manifested into the presence of this cheerful young man.

When we finally reached the YMCA, he asked if I wanted to get a beer. "No thanks," I said, and we parted.

Minutes later, the flight attendant arrived. That night, her brother gave me a motorbike tour through the city. The next day, I visited the National Palace Museum, said goodbye to my new friends, and flew home to the States.

Later, I wondered about that stranger. How had I managed to end up standing next to someone who spoke English, who knew how to get exactly where I wanted to go? Was he an angel? Or was he someone God guided to me in my time of need? I'll never know for sure.

> For to us a child is born, to us a son is given, and the government will be on his shoulders. And he will be called Wonderful Counselor, Mighty God, Everlasting Father, Prince of Peace.
>
> —ISAIAH 9:6 (NIV)

All I'm really sure of is that the Jesus I gave my life to all those years ago promised to never leave me. His Spirit has always been there to comfort and guide me. And on that day in Taiwan, I learned that He truly is the Wonderful Counselor, Mighty God, Everlasting Father, and Prince of Peace.

Miracle in Frankfurt
Sharon Beth Brani

I was desperate as I cried out in silent prayer, *Lord, please help me.* No one around me could hear my words, but I cried out anyway. I had nowhere else to turn, and I knew that without God's help, I was doomed to miss my plane home.

I pulled my new daughter's warm little body close to me as I staggered through the Frankfurt airport, weighed down by my baggage. All around me people hurried, oblivious, rushing to get to their gate.

The night before, my plane's ordinary fuel stop had unexpectedly turned into an overnight stay. Quickly, I had calculated the number of diapers I had with me, hoping that I would have enough to last me the extra hours. I already knew the number of formula-filled bottles I carried. It had all been carefully counted out while I was in Russia, preparing to travel back to the States with the six-month-old baby girl I had just adopted there. All planned and prepared. But suddenly the unexpected happened, and I was thrust into this crisis. The formula bottles were quickly dwindling, and I knew I had to get home soon. There was just one more flight from Frankfurt to Washington, DC, and I couldn't afford to miss it. That night I studied the airport map, not wanting to risk getting lost on my way to the gate.

My heart beat rapidly as I walked the busy thoroughfare that morning. I was completely exhausted. The adoption process in Russia had been long, and I'd been tired even before I began the journey home. Sweat trickled down my brow, and I swallowed my rising worry. I was alone, carrying much too much luggage, and didn't know how I'd ever make it to the gate in time for my flight.

I stopped and put down the brick-heavy brown travel bag. I moved the plastic bag carrying the hand-painted samovar—a metal pot used to boil water for tea—to my other arm, feeling some relief as I repositioned the weight. It was heavy and cumbersome. What had prompted me to buy it three days earlier in Russia? Much as I admired it then, now it just added to my problem. There was too much to carry for one single woman traveling alone. So many baby things along with my daughter, too. I had thought I could do it. Somehow, as I was packing for the trip, I had believed there would be a way. But now? Now I wondered how in the world I would ever make it to that distant gate.

> **Have I not commanded you? Be strong and courageous. Do not be afraid; do not be discouraged, for the LORD your God will be with you wherever you go.**
>
> —JOSHUA 1:9 (NIV)

I noticed my little brown-eyed treasure gaze up at me with curiosity, wondering what I was doing. With my right hand, I gently adjusted my newly adopted daughter in the carrier. *How precious. God, You are so good.*

It was a good thing that my big suitcase was already checked on the plane. But a baby in the infant carrier in front, a bag packed full of infant supplies, and the weighty black-and-pink samovar were well over my limit. I had no choice but to do it. *Just a little bit farther.* I just had to get to the gate in time. I glanced at my watch. *Walk. Keep walking*, I said to myself. There was no time to waste.

God. God, I need You now. Help me. I was weary. Absolutely exhausted. Feelings of panic rose within me. What was I to do? *Lord, You've carried me all through the international adoption. You've provided for all my needs. You've kept me safe every moment I've been out of the States. You protected us last night, when that terrifying banging came on our locked hotel door. Again and again You've been there. Now, help me, Lord.*

Then suddenly, as soft as the gentlest breeze, I sensed a response within: *Ask someone.*

But who? I glanced to my right and then to my left as fast-walking people of every description flowed around me. My eyes scanned the river of people, trying to catch someone's eyes. Everyone kept their own eyes forward, seemingly intent on where they were going. Serious. Focused. Determined. There was no time for a woman in distress. Especially not an obviously American woman.

But I asked. I spoke rapidly, trying to get attention. "Could you please—" But my words evaporated into thin air as the person hurried past me. I felt tears of exhaustion and a mounting panic press behind my eyes. *Ask someone. Someone. Someone. Anyone.*

Crucial minutes were ticking by. I had to get to that gate. We had to get on that plane to take us home. *Home. Home. Home.*

I put my bags down again and turned my body halfway around. Once more, I tried to catch someone's eyes, but no one even glanced my way.

There is no help for you, an inner voice of despair taunted me. *No help.*

God, I need You, I cried out silently. *Help me.*

Then I saw him. A quickly moving man without any bags.

"Excuse me," I stammered out, trying to get his attention. "Please—"

He passed to my left with not even the slightest glance my way.

Again, the tears pressed behind my eyes. But I was too weary, too desperate to even care if someone saw me crying.

One more time. Just try one more time, I thought.

I looked back to my left, and saw another man rapidly coming closer. He was slightly built, with light brown skin. His dark eyes met mine. "Do you need help?" he asked me.

"Yes. Yes, yes." The words tumbled out of me. Could this really be happening?

In one scoop, he picked up my two bags and resumed walking.

"Where are you going?" he asked.

I told him the gate and the time of my flight.

"You will make it," he reassured me. "We will get there on time."

Suddenly, I breathed easier. I quickly moved to keep up with my walking answer to prayer.

He spoke again, motioning to my little daughter.

> **Even to your old age and gray hairs I am he, I am he who will sustain you. I have made you and I will carry you; I will sustain you and I will rescue you.**
>
> —ISAIAH 46:4 (NIV)

GOD'S GIFT OF SIGHT
— Tez Brooks —

THE OPTIC NERVE contains more than a million nerve cells. Those, along with millions of rods and cones, help the human brain distinguish shapes and ten million different colors. The eye is the fastest muscle in the body, contracting in less than 1/100th of a second. In fact, because the eye can focus on up to fifty different objects per second, 80 percent of all learning comes through sight. The human eye is truly a unique and complex organ, allowing us to behold the beauty of God's creation.

"I have a little girl about her age. I'm going home to Hawaii to see her." He smiled the biggest smile I'd seen in a while.

He knew. He saw my need and he somehow knew the desperation of my situation.

Almost jogging after him, I soon saw the sign for my gate in the distance. Panting with relief, I kept going. *Thank You, God. Thank You, God.*

And then, suddenly, I was there. I stopped and turned. My bags were placed by my feet, but I couldn't see my friend. I glanced all around the growing crowd of people waiting for their flight. He was nowhere in sight. But there stood my bags. *I never had a chance to say thank you,* I thought.

Within a few minutes, the flight was boarding, and I lifted my bags to join the other passengers. My heart was still pondering. I was there. I had made it. God had brought me to the gate just in time.

I kissed the curly hair on the top of my little girl's head and whispered my thanks to the One Who Always Knows. Who always is there when we cry out to Him. Whether the stranger who helped me was an angel or simply a kind man, I still don't know. But I know I would never forget. It's been more than 30 years, and that intense experience of God still whispers its memory within my heart as if it had happened today. Because in a way, it did happen today. And it keeps happening. Over the years God has shown me over and over that He is faithful, even—especially—in our most desperate times.

God Showed Up

Patricia Cameron

For Elijah, God showed up in a whisper.

For me, God showed up on a motorcycle.

My car blew out a tire while driving through a not-so-safe small town on my way home from a funeral 6 hours away. I wasn't certain what had happened at first, because I heard no sound. The tire gauge alert, however, spoke loud and clear. My tire pressure had quickly dropped to 22 from a recommended 35. From there, the decline continued every few seconds.

I called friends who lived close by. No answer.

I tried to stay positive. *If I can make it to the gas station on the edge of town, it will be well lit, so at least I'll be safer.*

By the time I arrived, though, my car's PSI number had plunged to 9. My heart sank when I saw only darkness surrounding the station. *Why are they closed? It's only 10 on a Friday night.*

I had no choice but to pull up to the air pump and try to inflate the tire myself. That was a no-go, because the tire had deflated completely. Zero air in it.

As I stood by my car, wondering what to do next, I heard the roar of a motorcycle. A moment later I saw that the driver was heading straight for me, so I ran to my car's driver-side door and jumped inside. I wasn't taking any chances.

As the motorcyclist drove past, he shouted his reassurance: "I'm not going to hurt you!" He rode to the end of the parking lot, turned around, and came back to me. I cracked open my window as he stopped beside me, my heart lodged in my throat. My stress level shot to an alarming rate.

As he spoke, however, my anxiety began to dissipate. He told me that his name was Jeremiah and that he had seen me from his house close by. He knew that area of town was dangerous, so he came to help. "I told my wife, 'I'm going to go help that old lady.'"

> **As I was with Moses, so I will be with you; I will never leave you nor forsake you.**
>
> JOSHUA 1:5 (NIV)

OK, so that last part didn't help. No one had ever described me as an old lady before, at least not to my face. But he seemed sincere when he said he wasn't going to hurt me, so I said a quick prayer for protection and got out of the car.

My rescuer chatted in colorful language while changing my tire out for the spare. I chatted back, while at the same time keeping up a conversation with a friend on the phone. She had been home when I called, and as soon as I explained my predicament she had jumped in her own car and headed my way to help.

At one point, Jeremiah's head darted out from under the car seconds before the tire jack collapsed, and my concern shifted from my safety to his. But he kept working, and soon he'd secured the spare tire and loaded the old one in my car, all while sharing many of his life stories. I thanked him as we said our goodbyes.

When I told my story to another friend later that night, she recognized God's rescue right away. "God sent an angel to help you."

I disagreed at first. "He was no angel. I don't think angels talk like that."

But as I pondered my friend's words later, I changed my opinion. She'd seen the situation for what it was. Jeremiah means "appointed by God" or "God will exalt" in Hebrew. The Jeremiah who changed my tire may not have known it, but God had sent him to my rescue. He rode in on a two-wheeled chariot and embraced the task with determination and friendly conversation—and a few expletives thrown in.

> "Do not be afraid of them, for I am with you and will rescue you," declares the LORD.
>
> —JEREMIAH 1:8 (NIV)

God used that flat-tire experience to teach me a lesson. His protection came from someone I least expected, in the place I least expected to find it. I left in awe and appreciation for my God, who walks beside me when I am afraid.

I prayed. God delivered.

Make friends with the angels, who though invisible are always with you. Often invoke them, constantly praise them, and make good use of their help and assistance in all your temporal and spiritual affairs.

—Saint Francis de Sales

CHAPTER 3

Guarded by Invisible Angels

His Hand Upon Me 88
   Lori Rowe Summer, as told to
   Maggie Wallem Rowe

The Ride Home. 93
   Renee Mitchell

Delivered from Devastation 98
   Lori Stanley Roeleveld

Saved by an Angel? 103
   Renee Yancy

Slammed Yet Unscathed 107
   Diana DeSpain Schramer

His Hand Upon Me
Lori Rowe Summer, as told to Maggie Wallem Rowe

I stifled a yawn as I knocked on the door of my office building. I usually tried to catch a nap before reporting for the midnight shift. This Sunday, though, I'd just returned from visiting a friend's family in central Illinois. Maybe the noise of the office machines would keep me awake for the next eight hours.

Even though it was late April, the night air had grown chilly. I pulled on a light windbreaker as I waited for the door to open.

Quick steps sounded inside, and a face peered at me through the glass panel. Bonnie smiled as she swung the door open wide.

"Well, Lori, it's just you and me tonight," she said cheerfully as she locked the door again. "The other two girls called in sick."

Bonnie was my supervisor at this small firm in the Chicago suburb of Glen Ellyn. After only seven weeks on the job doing data entry, I still had lots of questions. Bonnie was always willing to help me.

This sort of work was new for me. I was enrolled as a sophomore at nearby Wheaton College but wasn't taking any courses that spring because I'd been accepted for a special summer program. A single mom in the community provided room and board in exchange for watching her daughter during the day. By working at night, I hoped to earn the tuition I needed for summer school.

Only six weeks left, I thought as I sat down at my machine in the middle of the room. I'd have a few days in California with my family, and then I would be off to Wheaton's Science Station. I couldn't wait.

The noise of the keypunch machine filled the room as I yawned again. It would be a long night.

As much as I loved my parents, I couldn't think of California as home. We had moved from upstate New York to San Bernardino just before my senior year in high school. I hated leaving all my friends. I chose to be miserable and made sure my parents knew it.

> Behold, God is my salvation. I will trust, and will not be afraid; for the LORD GOD is my strength and my song, and he has become my salvation.
>
> —ISAIAH 12:2 (ESV)

"Lori, you'll have to learn to depend on God just as Mom and I have," Dad would say gently. "He brought us here, and He'll take care of all of us."

Now I was a college student, really on my own. During my freshman year, my heart softened, and my anger subsided as God made Himself known to me through new friends and godly professors. At the beginning of my sophomore year, I prayed: "God, all my life I've depended on other people—my family, friends, guys I've dated. Teach me to depend on You and only You."

My thoughts roamed freely as I bent over my machine that April night of 1978. The work was routine and repetitious, but at least I had plenty of time to think and pray. I glanced at the clock on the far wall. 3:50 a.m. Almost time for my break.

Out of the corner of my eye, I caught movement near the front door. A man with a dirty white towel tied across his face was moving toward me, a gun in his left hand and a large laundry bag in his right.

Instantly alert, my chair scraped the floor as I pushed back. The intruder motioned with the gun for me to get up.

"Back room," he mumbled. "Move it."

Bonnie had been working in another room. Hearing voices, she reentered the central office, alarm written on her face.

The man herded us into the lunchroom and made us lie face down. He removed a wad of brown twine from the bag. Bonnie and I were both talking by now, trying to convince him to take our money and leave us alone. But he made it clear that he didn't want money; he intended to hurt us.

The intruder jerked my hands behind my back and bound my wrists and ankles with twine. He shoved Bonnie ahead of him into another room.

I was sitting near a back exit. *If I can just get my shoes off,* I thought, *maybe I can use my toes to free my ankles so I can run for help.* Wriggling my feet, I had kicked off my shoes and worked the twine off one ankle when the assailant hurried back into the room, cursing. He stooped, pulling the rope and knocking me over.

I heard the pounding of feet. *Run, Bonnie,* I mouthed silently. *Run!*

But the man had heard her, too. In one swift motion, he stepped into the outer office and fired a single shot. I heard a heavy thud. The assailant ran back to me and raised the revolver. I was trapped alone with someone who was about to kill me.

"Oh God, no. Oh God," I cried.

I'm going to heaven. When I open my eyes, I will be with Jesus.

In the next instant, something happened that I cannot explain. I felt what seemed like a large hand on the back of my head pushing me down into an unusual position. The pressure was sudden and startling.

There was a sound like an explosion. The force of the shot flattened me.

Time stood still. The next thing I remember was my ears ringing as I struggled to sit upright. Blinking and bewildered, I stared at the blood spreading across my chest. *Is this heaven?*

There was no sound in the room, no evidence of anyone else present. *I'm still alive,* I thought with wonder. *But I've been shot, and no one has come.*

Had the man left the building? With rising panic, I imagined him waiting for me outside. But an inner voice spoke to me quietly, reassuringly.

It's all right now, Lori. He's gone. Go for help.

I struggled to my feet but immediately collapsed. The bullet had shattered my left leg, and it wouldn't support my weight.

Must be broken, I thought. *All right, so I'll crawl.*

With my hands still bound beneath my back, I forced myself to one knee and crept into the main workroom, dragging my left leg behind me. Bonnie was on the floor facing me. I heard her exhale, and then she was still. It was up to me to summon help.

Spotting a push-button phone on the desk closest to me, I reached my bound hands around and knocked the receiver off

> **And I am sure of this, that he who began a good work in you will bring it to completion at the day of Jesus Christ.**
>
> —PHILIPPIANS 1:6 (ESV)

the hook. I pushed "O." Nothing happened. Remembering I needed an outside line, I tried again. Connected! I rested my ear on the receiver and choked out what had happened.

The compassionate operator stayed on the line with me until the police and ambulance arrived. As uniformed personnel filled the room I lay back, exhausted. "Thank You, God," I whispered over and over. A paramedic began checking my wounds. "Oh, thank You, Jesus!"

I learned later that the bullet had entered and exited my right arm, passed through the right side of my chest, and lodged in my left leg, shattering the tibia. Miraculously, no vital organs or nerves were damaged. The doctors were mystified by the strange path the bullet, fired at point-blank range, had taken.

As for Bonnie, the paramedics were unable to save her. The first shot fired had pierced her heart.

I don't know why my life was spared and Bonnie's was taken. But I do know that the God who patiently endured my anger in California, the God who went with me to college, was utterly faithful. I could depend on Him absolutely.

As I was wheeled out to the waiting ambulance, one of the paramedics leaned over me.

"I heard you thanking God in there," he said. "I'm a Christian, too. His hand was on you tonight."

It certainly was.

The assailant, James Free, was captured out of state, convicted after a jury trial, and given the death sentence by the state of Illinois for the murder of Bonnie Serpico and the attempted murder of Lori Rowe. Lori went on to graduate from Wheaton College in 1980 and presently lives in Lafayette, Indiana, where she is a leader in Bible Study Fellowship. She is the mother of five children and two grandchildren.

The Ride Home
Renee Mitchell

As soon as the pastor concluded the closing prayer, we were out the church doors. Lunch was in the oven and getting home was key to setting things in motion for a successful afternoon!

My son, Aaron, his wife, and their little son Austin—just a few weeks old—had come with us to Sunday morning service. We had asked if Austin could ride home with us, but after a short discussion it was decided that he was going to stay with his parents for the ride home. Although we didn't know it at the time, it was a wise decision.

It had begun to rain, and I jumped in the driver's seat. Larry, my husband, hopped in the front seat and Nikki, our daughter, got in the back. We were driving through the little town of Pleasant Hope, Missouri, just a few short miles from our home. The dreary day was making it a little harder for me to see, and it didn't help that the traffic was getting pretty congested. A lot of the churches in the area had just let out, and people were in a hurry to get to their destinations.

Right in the center of the community is a four-way stop sign. I stopped, waited my turn, and then proceeded through the intersection.

Something to my right caught my eye. I glanced in that direction and saw a truck approaching the stop sign—but it wasn't stopping. I looked left, but the other lane was full of cars.

No escape route there. The truck was headed right for us, and there was nothing I could do.

I heard myself say, "Oh, Jesus!" There was a terrible screeching sound and then a horrendous jolt. The impact was fast, hard, and violent, and then everything stopped.

I could hear the truck's engine running. It was so close, so loud, that it was like we were inside the motor. I remember reaching down and turning the key to shut off our van, thinking it was our vehicle.

The smell of oil and fluids from both vehicles filled the air, making me nauseous. The realization was sinking in that we had just been in a terrible accident.

As I looked around in a daze, it was like watching a movie. Though we were right in the middle of a busy intersection, everything had stopped. The people who had been driving were either running to help or staring to see what was to come.

Larry was yelling that he was OK and calling out our names, wanting to hear the same from Nikki and me. Nikki had been thrown over in the seat, but now she was sitting up and unbuckling her seat belt, checking herself to make sure she was good. I couldn't move at first. I ran my hand down the front of my chest where I had hit the steering wheel. I was OK. There was no pain, no sign of blood on anyone. *How in the world did we all come out of this OK?*

I couldn't help but notice there was nothing between the dash of our van and us. The van had airbags that should have deployed when the truck hit us, but they didn't. There had been nothing to keep the truck from throwing Larry into the dashboard as we spun around except our seat belts. Our injuries could have been so much worse.

The truck had hit us on the passenger side. The realization began to sink in. Nikki was in the middle seat, and had the baby been with us, he would have been right where the truck impacted. It was all smashed in, and to this day it makes me cringe to think of what could have happened if Austin's car seat had taken the force of that truck.

I looked over at the truck that hit us. An older gentleman and his wife were being helped from the wreckage of his vehicle. He seemed frail to me and very shaken up. He broke free from the group of people surrounding him and his wife and came over to us. He was terribly concerned about our well-being. He kept saying that he had been looking past the stop sign and didn't realize he had gone through it. I felt sorry for him. He was shaken and scared, and I, too, felt panic trying to creep in.

> **But let all who take refuge in you be glad; let them ever sing for joy. Spread your protection over them, that those who love your name may rejoice in you.**
>
> —PSALM 5:11 (NIV)

We heard the wail of sirens as police and ambulances headed our way. The town was so small that it only took minutes for them to arrive. After checking us out, they determined we were OK and made us all promise to go to the ER if anything changed. Other than the seat belt burns and some bumps and bruises that we weren't yet feeling, we were all in good shape. The EMT also noticed that no air bags had deployed and commented that he couldn't believe Larry and I weren't hurt worse. The driver and passenger in the other vehicle seemed OK as well.

Finally, we did everything we needed to do and left our van to be picked up by a wrecker, while our son came and drove us home. Lunch was a little late that day, and the prayer over it was a little long!

A few days passed and the bruises and soreness came as expected. We eventually did go in to be seen by a doctor. I had bruises on my chest from my seat belt and also where I'd hit the steering wheel, but other than that we were fine.

We later learned that the other driver's truck was totaled. Our van needed a few thousand dollars of repair. After the repairs were complete on the van, we went to the body shop to pick it up. The mechanic talked to Larry about the repairs that had been made. He said they had discovered that the air bags had inflated, but underneath the van, not in the passenger compartment where they should have been. He said he couldn't believe that we had escaped with such minor injuries.

As the events sank in, we all realized what the Lord had done. We envisioned His angels arranged around us, holding us from being thrown into a window or crushed by the damage from the truck. Whispering in our ears to let Austin ride home with his parents, for Nikki to sit in the middle of the back seat

> **The Lord himself goes before you and will be with you; he will never leave you nor forsake you. Do not be afraid; do not be discouraged.**
>
> —DEUTERONOMY 31:8 (NIV)

GOD'S GIFT OF SIGHT
— Linda L. Kruschke —

OF ALL THE modes of travel, trains offer the greatest opportunity to enjoy God's gift of sight. If one is seated by a window, trusting the train engineer to be in complete control of the journey, then hidden waterfalls, meadows of flowers, or spinner dolphins playing in a coastal sound are sights to behold. God's creation is full of beauty and wonder. If we allow Him to guide the journey called life while we relax and stop worrying about things we can't control, He will reveal the unexpected and the beautiful.

---

and not on the passenger side, for the stronger of the two of us to sit on the right side of the van. The steering wheel that hit my chest would have impacted Larry differently had he been driving, and the damage could have been worse.

To this day, I smile as I imagine the angels holding us back, tilting us forward, holding that truck so the impact wasn't as powerful as it could have been—and, last but not least, keeping the other drivers out of the way. From the ambulance and police station up the street to the wrecker service down the road, we were covered. It was a small town, and everything was right outside of that four-way stop.

If God hadn't gone before us, so many things could have gone wrong. But because He loves and protects us, He made a way in the middle of it all for us to come out on the other side.

Delivered from Devastation

Lori Stanley Roeleveld

"Call 911 for us!"

Three weeks before Christmas, my husband, Rob, raced inside shouting up the stairs to my second-floor office before dashing back outdoors. Call 911 for us? Why do we need 911?

My husband is a volunteer firefighter for the local department, where my father was fire chief for more than 51 years. As a carpenter, Rob is also a veteran of his own workshop-related emergencies. He isn't one to shout or run in a crisis. In fact, I was accustomed to Rob arriving at the dinner table with duct tape around a finger or two. Whenever I'd express concern, he'd dismiss any suggestion of medical care, saying, "It's just a scratch." Only once before had I seen him so agitated. Shortly before Christmas the year prior, he'd hurried into the kitchen, grabbed a towel, tossed me the car keys, and announced, "We're going to the emergency room." It was only on the drive I learned his hand had a run-in with his table saw. (He's healed now. Two fingers are a bit shorter but, thankfully, functional.)

Today was different. He didn't sound injured. We live on a busy road, so I wondered if there'd been a car accident. Grabbing my phone, I hurried down the stairs and out the door, annoyed to have no other details. It had to be bad, though, for him to want 911, so I dialed on my way.

The call connected as I hit the driveway and froze in place, horrified. Smoke billowed from our industrial-size garage—one side of which we rented to a mechanic and the other was my husband's woodshop. It was on fire and, from the look of it, fully engulfed just feet away from our house. The billows heading our way demonstrated that the wind was going in the worst direction. Having grown up in a firefighter family, I recognized a catastrophic fire when I saw one. We could be about to lose everything!

No stranger to crisis myself, nonetheless my voice started to shake as I provided details to the 911 operator. My father had died years earlier, but I wished he was here now. I recalled the one time I'd heard my dad's voice shaking on a call to 911. He'd fallen through a floor and was trapped under rubble ten feet down. I suddenly understood how he'd felt.

I knew Rob was near the garage but I couldn't see him, only smoke. I prayed as I called my adult son and daughter. Our son and his family share our home, and my daughter's family lives nearby. Then I called our church and asked my friend Maria to spread the word to pray. We live at the top of a hill in a small town just half a mile from the fire station. Before I hung up, the first firefighters arrived. At the sight of rescue arriving, I dissolved into tears.

These firefighters are as close to me as family, but they didn't stop to greet me, instead dashing past me and heading toward the flames. Fire trucks and hoses filled our driveway and then lined the street as far as I could see. A rescue team arrived and set up in the backyard to handle any on-scene injuries. The police directed traffic. Tankers from several other fire districts rolled up, all carrying water. My pastor told me later he tried to come to us, but from the bottom of the hill to the top, all he could see was emergency vehicles. He prayed.

My fear was not unfounded. These well-trained firefighters knew very well that one side of the garage was full of the wood my husband used in his business and the other, used by the mechanic, contained products that could easily become accelerants. They were prepared for a fully involved structure fire that could easily spread on a windy and dry December day.

> "Because he loves me," says the LORD, "I will rescue him; I will protect him, for he acknowledges my name. He will call on me, and I will answer him; I will be with him in trouble, I will deliver him and honor him."
>
> —PSALM 91:14–15 (NIV)

My son arrived from work and hugged me only long enough to ask if Rob was inside the garage or out. I could see Rob by then, talking with a deputy chief and the fire marshal. My daughter-in-law arrived, wanting to be there when my grandsons' school bus pulled up. Two women from church walked across the lawn and sat with me on the porch as we prayed for protection over the house, our neighbor's homes, and all the first responders.

I couldn't watch any longer. I was sure the woodshop would be destroyed, along with all my husband's equipment and his wood. How would he earn income? How would we pay our bills? Worse, I feared the mechanic would also lose his livelihood. What were we going to do?

Eventually, the fire chief, a dear friend, walked over to offer me a hug and assurance that they had the situation in hand and would keep the fire from spreading to our home and the neighbors' property. I recovered enough to bring water out for the firefighters, but I couldn't watch as good men and women battled a fire in my own backyard. My chest hurt, and I had nothing to offer by way of help but my prayers, so I continued to pray. Rob and I have been through many troubles together. I knew whatever the loss, God would see us through this, too.

> **So Shadrach, Meshach and Abednego came out of the fire. . . . The fire had not harmed their bodies, nor was a hair of their heads singed; their robes were not scorched, and there was no smell of fire on them.**
>
> —DANIEL 3:26–27 (NIV)

When the smoke cleared, however, even the seasoned firefighters used the word *miracle* to describe the limit of the damage. By then I'd learned Rob had been burning scraps in a barrel to one side of the garage. He'd doused it thoroughly, but a spark must have carried on the wind and set to smoldering, unnoticed, before the back corner of the garage burst into flames.

Fire took most of the back corner wall right down to the studs and frame, as well as parts of the roof and several items stored in a loft. The back corner is the section of the woodshop

Rob uses as a drying room for his inventory of live-edge wood. It would have been the ideal kindle for a conflagration, and it should have been, but it was as if an unseen hand had drawn a line for the fire to stop.

When I finally had the courage to walk back there, I was with my three-year-old grandson, who wanted "to see the big fire hole in Opa's shop." I couldn't believe my eyes when Rob pointed out that all those drying planks that should have gone up like tinder were intact. Three were singed on the ends, but that was all. The mechanic's side of the garage had water damage, but he lost nothing and Rob's tools and work area all survived.

At New Year's, we joined the firefighters for a luncheon. When I remarked at how quickly we had more firefighters on scene than I would have imagined available at that time of day, they also let me know that "coincidentally" there were an unusual number of firefighters at the station midday when my call came in from 911. I let them know that all my calls after 911 were for prayer.

I was not surprised to hear they, too, considered the limited damage miraculous. They wanted to credit my fire chief father, who entered heaven in 2019. They laughed and said that he probably started the fire engines and opened the bay doors! As capable as my dad was on this side of glory, I happily testified it was my *heavenly* Father's intervention that saved us from the worst. In fact, I assured them, if Dad could be here now, he would also tell them that God deserves all the credit for this miracle.

Thank God for 911 and well-trained firefighters. Thank God, above all, that He hears the prayers of His people.

Saved by an Angel?
Renee Yancy

It was a beautiful spring morning in upstate New York, with a sky the blue of a robin's egg, and I was on my way to work in Rochester. At the age of 23, I was a new Christian and still on my Christian "honeymoon." Maybe you know it—that period of time when you first become born again, when you pray for lights to turn green or for the rain to stop, and it happens. I sensed God's presence everywhere around me. I had come full circle in my life and finally felt as if I'd found my "home." I was in love with the Lord and feeling as if all the burdens of the world had fallen away from me. I was His, and He was mine.

I lived in the little burg of Brockport, New York, on the Erie Canal. It was the same town where I had attended college, obtained my nursing degree, and started my first nursing job at Lakeside Hospital. It had been at Lakeside where I met some young people who had something different about them. That something different turned out to be the joy of the Lord, and shortly after I met them, I became born again. Now I had a new position working with a federal organization, the Professional Standards Review Organization. I lived in a house with other like-minded Christian girls, and life was wonderful.

So there I was, driving the back roads in my little green '67 Mustang, heading out of Brockport toward Rochester. I had a worship tape in the cassette player playing at full volume and

I was singing my heart out to the Lord, lost in wonder and delight, without a care in the world.

The back road I was on had a railroad crossing. It was a dangerous one, because while it had flashing red lights and bells, there were no boom barriers to swing down and prevent you from driving onto the tracks when a train was coming.

I approached the crossing, singing away. In a fraction of a millisecond, three things happened all at once:

> **Before they call, I will answer.**
>
> —ISAIAH 65:24 (NIV)

My car began to cross the tracks.

I finally noticed the red flashing lights.

I looked left and RIGHT THERE was the locomotive engine.

In the next millisecond, I shot across the tracks, and the train roared by behind me. The drivers waiting in line on the other side of the crossing all turned their heads as one and gaped, their mouths open in shock as I sped by. It must have looked like a split-second action scene from a movie.

I pulled onto the shoulder and turned off the car, my hands shaking. I had been a split second from being obliterated by the train. I had almost lost my life. All I could say, over and over, was, "Thank You, Lord. Thank You, Lord. Thank You, Lord."

I hadn't heard the bells. I hadn't heard the train's horn as it approached the crossing. I foolishly had my music playing too loud, and I wasn't paying close attention. I sat in my Mustang and shuddered as the image of the huge locomotive engine looming in my car window replayed endlessly in my mind. I must have given the locomotive engineer a heart attack.

Then my shock and relief gave way to another visual image: the Lord delightedly watching me as I sang to Him at the top of my lungs, totally unaware of my looming destruction. I felt as if He had chuckled indulgently and said, "Oh, Renee, Renee, Renee," then turned to one of His angels and said, "Get down there and hold that train back."

I knew then that the Lord holds the days, hours, minutes, and milliseconds of our lives in His hands.

Seven years later, I realized this anew. Now married, I had a two-year-old daughter and fraternal twin boys, who had recently been weaned at the age of 4 months. The ladies of my church had planned a day at Castaic Lake in southern California and my husband urged me to go and get out of the house with my daughter for a day of fun and fellowship.

So I packed a lunch with special treats and another bag with her floaties, the sunscreen, towels, sand toys, and all the things we'd need to make her first day at the beach a memorable one. When we arrived, a sign at the entrance announced that there was a mollusk growth going on in the water. Although it made the water somewhat murky, it was harmless and safe to swim in. I parked near the beach and started to unpack the car.

We'd been there barely a minute when one of my friends said, "Looks like they're going in to rescue someone."

We watched the young lifeguard race over the sand, sprint into the water, and pull up a little girl.

My daughter, Sarah.

I'd never been to this beach before. I didn't know it had lifeguards. I didn't know it was the kind of beach that sloped quickly down to deep water. All I knew was that while I was busy unpacking everything I had brought to make her day special, my

2-year-old daughter, the heart of my heart and the light of my eyes, had wandered unseen to the beach, entered the water, lost her footing, and was drowning 50 feet away from me.

Shaken, I ran to the lifeguard holding Sarah. "I saw her fingers above the water," he said. "Another second or two and it would have been too late." Because the water was murky, he wouldn't have been able to find her quickly.

> **The eyes of the LORD are everywhere, keeping watch on the wicked and the good.**
>
> —PROVERBS 15:3 (NIV)

The lifeguard gave Sarah some oxygen. She was perfectly fine, just a bit scared by all the attention.

My friends were all watching me. "Do you want to go home?" asked one.

"No," I said, "it's OK. We're here, let's stay."

We did. I don't remember much about the rest of that afternoon. I think I was in a state of shock. It wasn't until I arrived home and told my husband what had happened that it hit me. As I was putting my daughter to bed, I started weeping, realizing how close I had come to losing her. At that moment, I felt the Lord speak softly to me: *I answer before you even know you need to call.*

Had He sent one of His angels to hold Sarah up long enough for the lifeguard to see her fingers above the water?

Once again, the Lord had shown me that He holds our lives in His hands, the days and hours and seconds, down to the milliseconds, protecting us and keeping us safe. He is always watching over us, and we can infinitely trust Him.

Slammed Yet Unscathed
Diana DeSpain Schramer

My 9-year-old granddaughter, Mila, and I were driving to my home for our monthly weekend together. It was a picture-perfect September day—not a cloud in the sapphire sky, with the temperatures in the mid-seventies. As usual, Mila chattered nonstop from the passenger side in the back seat. For the entire hour-long drive, she regaled me with stories and updates about her school, friends, activities, and exciting new art projects.

As we neared my city, we were starving, so we decided to stop at Arby's. As we passed through the first stoplight, the thought occurred to me to turn there. But instead, I decided to go to the next stoplight, reasoning that both routes to Arby's were about the same distance. Looking back, I can't help but feel that Mila's and my angels were attempting to intervene in what they knew lay ahead.

It was now around 2 p.m., and the four-way intersection was jammed with vehicles. I pulled into the left-turn lane to wait for the green arrow. Mila and I were debating our menu options when the green arrow appeared.

I accelerated and turned left. We were about three-fourths into the turn when, out of nowhere, a pickup truck came hurtling toward us in the oncoming lane that had a red light. In that brief second I thought if I could just speed up, it would miss us. But I didn't get the chance.

I heard a sickening, metal-crunching thud as the force of impact sent us spinning like a top. Then, just as quickly, we came to an abrupt stop, now facing in the opposite direction from where we were headed.

For the first few seconds, the only thing I was aware of was my galloping heart and the blood thundering in my ears. Still gripping the steering wheel, I stared straight ahead in shock.

Then I remembered...

Mila!

I unfastened my seat belt and twisted around, panicked. Mila was still in her booster seat and belted in, looking around in a daze at the melee outside my car in the middle of the congested, now frenzied intersection.

"Honey, are you OK?"

She turned to face me as if she were in a trance. For a long couple of seconds, she sat looking at me, wide-eyed and mute. Finally, recognition dawned in her brown eyes, and they immediately filled with tears. "I think so," she said, her voice small and quivering.

"Are you sure? Did you hit your head on the window or anything?" *I don't see any blood. Is she really OK? Did she hit her head? What if she has a concussion?* My jackhammering heart felt like it was going to explode.

"I don't think so. I think I might have bumped my arm, though."

I then heard a knock on my window. When I rolled it down, a man with a cell phone to his ear said, "Is everyone all

> **Whoever conceals their sins does not prosper, but the one who confesses and renounces them finds mercy.**
>
> —PROVERBS 28:13 (NIV)

right? I'm trying to call 911, but they dropped my call!" He punched the keys with his finger.

I told him we were both OK. He shouted into his phone and then hung up, cursing. Throwing his hands in the air, he said, "I can't get through!"

I reached for my phone and dialed 911, thankful for something to focus on. Someone immediately answered, and I somehow maintained the presence of mind to give the dispatcher the details. They assured me that help was on the way, instructing me to stay in my vehicle until they arrived.

I turned around in my seat again to check on Mila, who was still uncharacteristically quiet. She had unbuckled her seat belt and moved to the center of the back seat, leaning forward between the seats to be closer to me. By now, I could hear sirens screaming from all directions.

"Honey, are you sure you're not hurt?" I looked her over again, alert for any sign of injury, and was relieved to still not see any blood.

She shook her head. We sat in silence, both of us looking around, dazed. Then she said, her voice small and shaking, "Grandma, can we pray?"

I had been praying in my heart the entire time, but it had never occurred to me to pray out loud together with Mila. "Out of the mouths of babes," as her great-grandma Schramer used to say.

"Of course we can pray." I took her hand in mine and closed my eyes. "Dear Jesus, thank You so much for protecting us. Please help us through all of this." My voice cracked as the shock started to wear off and the enormity of what had happened, and what could have happened, began to sink in.

I opened my eyes and saw the young man who had hit us sitting down on the curb, his elbows on his knees, holding his head in his hands. He looked to be the same age as my son, Mila's dad. "And please help the young man who hit us. We pray that he's not hurt. We love You, Jesus. Amen."

Mila and I sat silent, still holding hands, watching the utter chaos swirling around us. Police officers were directing the traffic around my vehicle sitting in the center of the hectic intersection. Firefighters swarmed around, steering pedestrians away from the scene; paramedics attended to the young man who had hit us, who was speaking and appeared to be uninjured. I was struck, though, by the calm and silence inside my car. As if in the eye of a hurricane, Mila and I were enveloped in complete peace, a peace that only God can provide, a peace that was incomprehensible given the circumstances.

> **The LORD will watch over your coming and going both now and forevermore.**
>
> —PSALM 121:8 (NIV)

Suddenly, my door flung open. A man introduced himself as a member of the fire department. After asking Mila and me a couple of times if we were OK, and feeling assured that we were, he said, "We need to get you both out of the vehicle. One of my guys will escort you through the traffic and around the debris."

Mila and I gathered what we could of our belongings and then followed the fireman over to the curb and sat down. Within seconds, a police officer approached me with a clipboard and paperwork to fill out for the accident report. My hands were shaking so much I could barely hold the pen. Traffic was still a swarming quagmire, with people in the passing vehicles gawking at Mila and me and the whole scene as they were directed through the intersection and around my mangled car.

Another police officer came over and asked how we were feeling, and then stayed and engaged Mila about a game on her iPad while I managed to complete the paperwork. Soon Mila was back to her talkative, animated self as they shared stories about the game.

After handing the clipboard back to the police officer, I looked up and saw my car for the first time. The right rear quarter panel along with the tire was smashed deep into my trunk. If the pickup truck had hit us a few inches to the left, it would have hit my gas tank; a few inches to the right, it would have hit the door where Mila had been sitting.

The first fireman who had talked to us walked over and again asked how we were feeling. He assured me that if we had any injuries that they would have been apparent by now. He then looked at my car and said, "There's no way you're driving that car again. You'll need to get all of your things out of it before the tow truck takes it away."

He would not allow Mila and me to enter the congested intersection. Instead, he instructed a young fireman to retrieve our items, which took him three trips. With everything accumulated around us, including Mila's suitcase, Mila and I looked like refugees sitting at the side of the road.

I caught movement to my right out of the corner of my eye. Handcuffed and flanked by police officers, the young man who had hit us was looking over at Mila and me, his wide eyes filled with sorrow. When our eyes met, he called over, "Ma'am, I am so, so sorry." He started to cry. "I am so very sorry."

He had run a red light, totaled my car, and could have injured or killed Mila, someone else, me, even himself. Yet all I could see was a young man my son's age whose remorse was palpable. My heart melted, filling with compassion. "It's OK," I said to him, nodding. Through fresh tears, he dipped his head in gratitude and attempted a sad smile. Police officers then helped him into the back of a squad car and they drove away.

A few minutes later, one of the EMTs informed me about the cause of the accident. The driver had become distracted when he saw a bee in his truck. Highly allergic, he panicked and tried to get it out. Why he was arrested, I do not know.

The tow truck arrived, and the driver loaded what was left of my car on the flatbed. I could barely breathe as I watched him pull away with the pile of twisted, crumpled metal while Mila and I walked away without a bump, bruise, cut, or scratch.

All—and only—by the grace and presence of God and His garrison of angels.

We never need to feel that we are alone or unloved in the Lord's service because we never are. We can feel the love of God. The Savior has promised angels on our left and our right to bear us up. And He always keeps His word.

—Henry B. Eyring

CHAPTER 4

God Sends His Comfort

Angels with Feathers 116
   B. J. Taylor
When God's Eyes Twinkled at Me 122
   Roberta Messner
Chasing Dad 127
   Deb Gorman
Koda 134
   Elsa Kok Colopy
Angel in a Winter Storm 139
   Leone F. Byron
Midair Meeting 144
   Angela J. Kaufman

Angels with Feathers
B. J. Taylor

The bright red numerals on the digital clock read 3:35 a.m. when I was startled awake.

"What was that?" I sat up in bed. The noise I'd heard sounded like splashing.

"Come here and look," my husband, Roger, said. He was standing at the window, the blinds parted.

I threw back the covers and rushed to his side. A loud noise broke the quiet of the night. *Quack, quack.* There were ducks in the pool. That had happened a few times before, but always during the day, and always one male and one female. They'd glide quietly, dip their heads into the water, then swoop off. But these ducks splashed around and made a huge racket. And in the middle of the night.

"Look," I whispered. "There are three of them."

"It's a sign," Roger said.

"Yes," I barely breathed.

For years, my husband Roger and I had two cats in our home. One was a marmalade color who we'd named Red, and the other we called Diamond after we saw the markings on her gray-and-white face. For five years the cats played together, slept curled up tight in a wicker basket, and licked and groomed each other until their coats shined. Then we added a rambunctious Golden Lab puppy named Rex. The cats were an energetic welcoming committee when Rex bounced in.

Our cute puppy grew to a healthy 80 pounds and towered over the cats, but that never scared off Red, who sauntered past with head held high. When this gorgeous cat began to lose weight and his fur became matted, we took him to the vet. Tests determined the diagnosis. He was diabetic. We bought special food and filled prescriptions for insulin.

"Come on, Red, time for your shot," Roger called out from the kitchen every morning. Red jumped right up on the counter for the insulin that managed the disease. We repeated the routine every night.

Ten years seemed to whiz by as our trio of furry friends filled our home with noise and laughter, especially the turbo-charged energy of a Lab. When it kicked in, you couldn't stop it. Rex zoomed around the furniture so fast our heads spun, and we'd laugh until our sides hurt. Diamond and Red took up position on one of the stairs leading to the second floor and watched Rex, their tiny heads bending one way and then the other as they followed the zooming of a crazy puppy.

> **But they who wait for the LORD shall renew their strength; they shall mount up with wings like eagles; they shall run and not be weary; they shall walk and not faint.**
>
> —ISAIAH 40:31 (ESV)

One year, about a week before Christmas, we saw Rex with a wrapped present from under the tree. He held the package down with his paw while he methodically tore off the festive paper with his teeth. "Rex, what's this you have?" I came up beside him. He spit pieces of the wrapping paper off to the side. I grabbed what was left of the paper, the ribbon, and the gift. He hadn't torn into the bag of treats yet. "Rex," I admonished, "you have to wait for Christmas." He stared up at me with a quizzical look, a piece of paper hanging out the side of his mouth.

> **For the LORD comforts his people and will have compassion on his afflicted ones.**
>
> —ISAIAH 49:13 (NIV)

His antics promised there was never a dull moment and the comfort of all three of our animals made our house a loving home. Then one night Diamond had a stroke and was gone. Less than a year later, Red was gone too.

The house felt empty without the meows from Red on the counter and the warm purrs from Diamond nestled next to my pillow, so we adopted another dog. A small one this time, a rescue named Charlie Bear. He came with some issues, and it was tough to get through it all at first. Charlie Bear thought he was a big dog in a little body, and Rex let him think that all he wanted. He taught Charlie Bear the ropes, like how to alert us to squirrels that jumped from tree to tree or possums and raccoons that walked along the top of the brick wall that surrounded the backyard. And especially to ducks that landed in our backyard pool.

Just eight months after Charlie Bear joined our home, Rex got sick. Very sick. He couldn't keep anything down. He lost a lot of weight, had no energy, and walked around in a daze. Even Charlie Bear couldn't perk him up to play. I'd creep downstairs to check on Rex sleeping in his room, sneaking past Charlie Bear asleep in his den. I'd trudge back up the stairs with fresh tears on my face. After another round of visits to the vet, trying all sorts of different food, even Ensure to put on weight, the vet said the word *cancer*.

Rex's pleading eyes told me all I needed to know. I had to let my beloved friend go. It was heart wrenching to feel Rex go limp in my arms. I wrapped him in his favorite blanket and kissed him goodbye, then left the vet's office sobbing. My beautiful Golden Lab would never come home again, and I couldn't stand the pain. Did I do the right thing? Should we have put Rex through painful tests and prolonged his life? Grief consumed me. I'd lost so much in the past year. First Diamond, then Red, both fifteen years old, and now eleven-year-old Rex. Why did I have to lose him too?

The night we put Rex to sleep, not even the soft, nuzzling nose of Charlie Bear could stop the torrent of tears. "God," I whispered in prayer, "please help me to know we did the right thing, and that Rex is free from suffering. That he's in your loving care."

We put Charlie Bear to bed in his den near the window in the family room and I dragged myself up the stairs to bed. Roger hugged me close.

Sleep was elusive, and I tossed and turned, torturing myself with regrets and wondering if I could ever love a pet fully and deeply ever again. Then the sudden splashing in the pool startled me and I joined Roger at the window.

One male duck and one female duck swam together on the left side of the pool.

On the right was a stately, strong, sentinel male duck.

Roger and I stood mesmerized. I was surprised Charlie Bear didn't wake up and bark. These ducks made quite an announcement of their presence.

The two ducks on the left stuck close to each other the whole time, like Diamond and Red used to do. They dived, dunked, and groomed each other and seemed to have a marvelous, rollicking, grand time while emitting moderate quacking noises.

The beautiful, brightly colored mallard on the right held his head high and rigid and swam in tight circles. Confident. Proud. His quacks were pronounced, sharp, and loud, like Rex's bark used to be.

Quack, quack, the ducks announced. It was almost as if I could hear the message they conveyed. *We're over the Rainbow Bridge. We're here to tell you we're all together and everything is OK.*

After a while, the ducks flew off into the night. Roger and I went back to bed and I wondered, as sleep overcame me, if three ducks in the pool were just a coincidence.

The next morning I rose early and sat at my desk in Rex's room. Suddenly, the lone mallard returned. He swooped in low and landed in the pool just outside my window. He swam a bit, then hopped out and sat on the deck. He looked straight at me and quacked for a long time. Through my tears, I felt an immense comfort, as if Rex was telling me, *I know you miss me. But it's OK. You did the right thing.*

My beloved friend was no longer suffering. I closed my eyes and whispered, "Thank you, God, for the answer to my prayer." The duck flapped his wings and soared into the sky.

I had received not one but two opportunities to feel God's love for all creatures. The unusual arrival of the three ducks brought me healing that night, something I desperately needed, and hope for a future without overwhelming grief.

It was a message I will never forget, delivered by three quacking angels sent from heaven with wings made of feathers.

When God's Eyes Twinkled at Me

Roberta Messner

Not a creature was stirring in my hospital room that early December evening. The facility was in Covid lockdown. The only faces I saw wore masks, their eyes belonging to total strangers. I missed my family. My friends. My little town. The old log cabin I called home. The dearly familiar people and places that would never be mine again unless through a miracle I could regain my independence.

I'd taken a terrible tumble and fractured my hip, pelvis, and femur. I was caged in a bed with four side rails when the cell phone under my pillow rang.

"I'm one of your readers, Roberta," a lady was saying. "I heard about your fall. The *Guideposts* grapevine, you know." I did know. Readers with sweet voices and promises of prayers had found me for over three decades. None had said anything like this. She spoke in the confidential whisper reserved for close friends. Oh, how I needed one! "When I was talking to God today, I saw a picture of you in my mind. You were sitting at a table in your cabin, writing a story for us. It was the most sacred scene. God never took His eyes off you. He was smiling. That's not all, Roberta. It was His eyes! They positively twinkled in delight."

God can't *be delighted with* you, *Roberta.* If He was, why had He allowed this to happen? I'd never been so broken in my life. But the lady's words refused to leave me, playing over and over like a tape in my head as I drifted off to sleep. When the nurses came in to reposition me, I realized I'd been dreaming. Not the visions-of-sugarplums variety. I vaguely remembered many hands holding objects like a screwdriver, a spatula, a wrench, a stethoscope. There were no faces, but of this I was certain: they were connected to the warmest hearts, ones that longed to use the talents unique to them to help others. A pair of eyes surveyed the storybook scene. Someone watching over it all, guiding, and oh, so pleased at the peace-filled sight.

The eyes twinkled.

I slept in fits and starts the rest of the night, snowflakes shivering at my window. When dawn broke, my physical therapist bounded through the door of my isolation room for our morning session. I was no match for her positivity. "I'll never be able to go home," I'd wailed to her countless times. "My cabin's no hospital. I live alone. It just can't be. There's too much to do. Besides, it's *Christmas.*"

> **Now you are the body of Christ, and each one of you is a part of it.**
>
> —1 CORINTHIANS 12:27 (NIV)

The phone call and the dream had been so compelling that I found myself telling her about them. The ridiculous part about God's twinkling eyes when he saw me at my computer. As I described my dream to her, I remembered the oddest part—in the middle of all the activity, a pair of hands with open palms stretching upward, doing nothing at all.

My therapist leaned over my bedrail, her dark, sweet-smelling curls brushing my cheek. We'd talked some about my decades-long nursing career. How I loved helping others, but hated to trouble folks for my own needs more than anything.

"Your dream makes perfect sense, Roberta," she told me. "You've always been the helper. This time it has to be different." She cradled my hands inside her own, her eyes now dancing. "All those hands in your dream? God's lining up your angels." The more she talked, the surer she sounded. "Those open hands are *yours*, Roberta! God's teaching you a new way to give—and to receive. *At Christmas!*"

I did go home not long after that, and what I found was my cabin bedecked in utter Christmas magic—adapted for broken me by a cast of angels. A hospital bed and the requisite equipment occupied the center of the floor, but center stage went to a vintage department-store Santa my sister had recruited from her attic. He moved his arms in welcome as the ambulance staff rolled me inside to the warmth of a crackling fireside. "I've never taken a patient to a place like this," the driver declared.

Promises from the hands of folks from all walks of life awaited me. This twenty-first century body of Christ offering their talents with a spirit of utter joy until total restoration was mine. It was an embarrassment of riches. A mechanic changed the oil in my car and checked the air in my tires to ensure that follow-up visits to doctors were safe. Neighbors doubled their party menu so my sister-caregiver and I would have a holiday celebration of our own across the road. The wife of a former patient brought me a tin of homemade candies and an assortment of decorative containers—something festive to send home with my visitors! A local restaurant owner brought fresh vegetables. The postal carrier delivered get-well cards inside my cabin. My home-care physical therapist climbed a ladder to fix my ceiling light so I could begin to write again. A local vet sent a Goldendoodle for a visit to cheer me.

One of the dearest offerings involved a medical equipment agency. When my cabin entrance was too narrow for a wheelchair to pass through, they were thrilled to take on the project of creating a smaller chair. On Christmas Eve, I texted them a photo of my chair in my cabin doorway with plenty of room to spare. They wrote right back: "Our best Christmas present ever!"

One of my most precious offerings came from a lady who'd helped me around the cabin prior to my fall. Recovering from addiction, she didn't own a vehicle. Yet she trekked four miles round-trip in the freezing December air to find me a pair of stockings that would slip onto my swollen leg with ease. I couldn't help but notice that the bag held packaging for stockings of four different sizes. I tallied up the cost. It had taken a full day's pay for her to buy them.

The old Roberta would've protested, but I remembered the dream, the open hands that belonged to me, the lesson about receiving that had come just in time for Christmas.

"Unbelievable!" I said, playing along with the Christmas magic. "What brand is this?"

> **For the entire law is fulfilled in keeping this one command: "Love your neighbor as yourself."**
>
> —GALATIANS 5:14 (NIV)

GOD'S GIFT OF SIGHT
— Eryn Lynum —

GLIMPSING A FIELD illuminated by fireflies on a summer night, one can contemplate the external representation of God's design of inner light. In a firefly, a sophisticated reaction between a luciferase enzyme and a luciferin molecule creates a flash of light—a living, organic reaction that shines through the darkness Similarly, God has placed living light into His children in the form of faith in Jesus. As He explained in John 8:12 (NIV), "I am the light of the world. Whoever follows me will never walk in darkness, but will have the light of life."

My worker, who had nothing—yet had everything—couldn't wait to tell me. She was so excited to have something to give. "They just came out with them, Berta. They're called *A Perfect Fit.*"

All these angelic gestures, an outpouring of God-given gifts, were so natural that nothing seemed to be an inconvenience. My own receiving hands knew a new kind of joy. And the mechanical Father Christmas who guarded my bed, watching it all? His eyes really did twinkle. Like our Heavenly Father who arranged every bit of it.

Chasing Dad

Deb Gorman

"You found him?" I gripped the phone with a trembling hand.

"Yes. His debit card was used in Idaho."

"Idaho?"

"Yeah. Here's the name of the place. It's a small motel and gas station on the highway. You'll want to cross the border at Lewiston and travel south. And here's his plate number."

I scribbled the information on the back of an envelope. "OK. Thanks, cuz. Sure glad you work for the police department. We're leaving right now."

"Take it easy. I don't want to have to find you, too."

"Right." I hung up the phone and turned to my husband, who'd just arrived home from work. I'd called him and said Dad had been reported missing by his daily coffee cronies. For Dad to be gone from his apartment for two days was unusual for him, and I didn't think he'd just leave without telling me. My husband and I both left work in the middle of the day to begin the search.

"Here's where we're going." I pointed to the envelope.

Ten minutes later we were on the road, traveling from our home in central Washington State to somewhere in Idaho.

My mind traveled back in time as we zoomed down the highway. My family had endured so much in the last decade. The deaths of my younger brother and only sister within 5 years of each other, plus my parents' divorce and all the baggage that went along with it. I'd divested myself of my faith during that long desert, intending to take a leaf out of Elijah's book and run away. I'd forgotten, though, about the end of Elijah's journey—he thought the path would take him *away* from God, but later found he was running straight into His arms. "And after the fire there was the sound of a gentle whisper" (1 Kings 19:12, NLT). That verse, once a favorite, was now hidden somewhere in the shards of grief, lying deep in the leftovers of my soul.

And now it seemed my dad was far away, running like Elijah, trying to escape the emotional fallout from the devastating loss of two adult children and his own messy divorce.

Somewhere inside me a voice whispered, telling me where he might be headed. And that voice scared me. I had to find him—if I didn't, I knew I'd lose him, too.

Hours later, in the pitch dark, we inched along a two-lane mountain highway. I was glad it wasn't the dead of winter. We didn't know how far we had to go, so we kept moving, hoping to get a break—maybe a sign on the highway announcing the name of the place where his debit card had been used. No such luck.

I hadn't prayed for a long time, derailed from God-conversations by tragedies and playing the blame game with Him. But now I was running out of hope. What in the world were we thinking, jumping into the car and driving to who knows where? We had no idea where we were—this was before GPS and smartphones. So I swallowed hard and whispered just one word, hoping someone was listening. "Help."

After a few more miles, we pulled off at an exit and headed for a mini-mart with one gas pump. Another building was nearby, but we paid no attention to it.

My husband filled up the tank, then swung our Jeep around to get back on the highway.

Then it happened. My Elijah moment.

Our headlights lit up a motel sign and something else. A familiar-looking pickup. I grabbed the envelope off the dash and verified the plate number.

"Is it him?" My husband grabbed the envelope from me and compared it to the one on the pickup. "It is. Come on, let's go."

"Wait." It occurred to me that in the rush to make sure my father was safe, I had no idea what I would say when I found him. "What excuse are we going to give him for being here? I mean, he's my dad, for crying out loud. He's an adult. He has a right to go where he wants, right?"

> You see me when I travel and when I rest at home. You know everything I do.
>
> —PSALM 139:3 (NLT)

"Of course. But not to just disappear without saying anything to you."

"He doesn't answer to me."

"Do you want to turn around and go back home?"

That put it into perspective, big time. "No, I guess not. But you'd better help me do the talking."

We entered the motel. To our right was a restaurant and gift shop. We stepped to the desk and asked for his room number, not thinking it would be given to us. I hated the thought of spilling my anxiety to a complete stranger, trying to explain why it was so important.

But the clerk obliged, and soon we stood outside my father's door.

I knocked.

The door opened a crack. Dad's eyebrows climbed to his hairline. "What in tarnation are you two doing here?"

"I might ask you the same question. Can we come in?" I tried not to be dismayed at his tone. He clearly did not want us here.

He opened the door wider and turned on his heel, sitting at a small table in the corner. We followed and sat. Dad and I stared at each other for a lifetime.

His gaze slid away from mine.

"Are you staying the night here?" I asked.

"Yes."

"Then what?" I had an idea, but I wanted him to say it.

"Going to Missoula in the morning."

"Missoula. Why?" Again, I knew.

He didn't answer, but his tear-filled eyes shouted at me.

"We're getting a room. We'll go with you."

"You don't have to do that."

"But we are."

I gave my husband a side glance and saw him nod in agreement.

"I'll be right back," I told them. As I opened the door to go down to the desk and make arrangements, I heard my husband ask a question I couldn't quite make out. I turned.

Dad's face had blanched, gazing at me from across the room. "Hadn't thought of it that way."

I shut the door, not wanting to know.

After a sleepless night, we had breakfast in the motel restaurant, then piled into our two vehicles and headed east to Missoula. Arriving around noon, we pulled into the Holiday Inn—*the* Holiday Inn, the one that I had understood intuitively was my father's destination—and parked.

We stepped out to the parking lot and stood in silence, not really knowing what to do next.

Dad decided for us. "Let's go in."

My husband stayed with the vehicles, giving Dad and me some space.

We stood in the motel lobby for a few minutes, like tourists at a cheap sideshow, gawking at guests coming and going. I knew Dad and I were both wrestling with the same questions that had haunted us for a decade, but they remained unvoiced.

What had it been like for my younger sister when she'd arrived here from her Seattle-area home on March 25, 1989, the day she'd decided to leave the world—and us—behind?

Did the clerk who'd checked her in have any inkling of her plan?

Did she think of us in her last moment?

To this day those questions remain in the drawer of the unanswerable.

We stood in the lobby, surrounded by memories, unsure of what to do next. Should we stay? Go farther into the hotel? Leave?

Finally, Dad decided. "Let's go."

We exited and strolled across the parking lot to our cars. Standing in the gentle breeze, silence closed us in. I watched smiling people towing luggage behind them, no doubt enjoying a getaway. I longed to join them instead of shuffling through these harsh memories.

Leaning on my vehicle, I glanced at Dad the same moment he looked my way.

He gave me a small, weary smile. "She's not here."

My heart cracked again. "No, Dad, she's not. Let's go home."

He nodded and took a last look at the motel. The final place on this earth that my sister's always-stylish shoes had touched.

We decided that my husband would drive Dad's pickup and he'd ride with me. It would give us a chance to talk. As we rolled out of the parking lot, my thoughts bounced around like a herd of crickets, first one way, then another. But I noticed a through line in the midst of the chaos.

Even though I'd allowed my faith to derail over the years, God was still on my track. He'd heard my plea for help when I needed to find Dad, just that one word. And He hadn't needed to travel far to answer me, because He was in the car with us, had been in the motel room in Idaho with Dad, and in that parking lot in Missoula when we'd arrived.

> **After the wind there was an earthquake, but the Lord was not in the earthquake. And after the earthquake there was a fire, but the Lord was not in the fire. And after the fire there was the sound of a gentle whisper.**
>
> —1 KINGS 19:11–12 (NLT)

And hardest of all for me to acknowledge was this—that He'd been in that room with my sister all those years ago. It had been inconceivable to me, for so many years, that God had been there and had not stopped it. But now I saw the truth. God's extravagant love is not changed by what we do with it, or how fast and far we run to get away from it. It just is. And always will be.

God's constant presence.

Dad wasn't the only one who was on his way back home. I knew that somehow we'd both be OK.

Koda

Elsa Kok Colopy

I had no idea how hard it would be.

When God set it in our hearts to adopt, I couldn't have guessed where the journey would take us. We had launched our first four kiddos into adulthood and sensed God was starting us on a brand-new adventure. It just didn't quite play out like we thought it would.

To begin with, we were open to adopting one child, and God brought four. We felt we were too old for special-needs parenting, and he gave us a nonverbal son who will be with us all of our days. We didn't think international adoption was even an option, and God took us to Haiti, where we fell in love with three of our babies. We doubted we could handle adopting an older child and God brought a beautiful 11-year-old girl with a significant history of trauma.

Well then.

At the end of all our doubts and fears, we were the proud parents of four adopted littles and four grown children.

Our youngest child came to us at birth, as she was adopted domestically. When she was three years old, our three Haitian kiddos came home, all within four months of one another. Like bringing home triplets, that season of life was filled with constant chaos, sleepless nights, and attempting to discern needs while overcoming language barriers.

To say it was challenging was an understatement.

As the mama bear, I lived in a constant state of exhaustion. My children were overwhelmed, out of their element, fearful, and grieving. Our 11-year-old had been told horrible things would happen to her in our care. For the first 4 months of her time with us, I slept in her room with the lights on. For the next 3 months, I stayed with her until she fell asleep and then carefully inched my way through the darkness, praying she wouldn't wake. The others required a similar level of intense care. Thankfully, my husband and I had been trained in attachment. We knew we would have to meet little needs over and over again, like you do with a newborn, in order to build a sense of trust and connection with our children.

It took everything we had.

Slowly, steadily, the attachment began to build, but it was a constant outpouring of self, of care, of time, of commitment, of food and play and love, love, love.

Many mornings, evenings, noontimes, I called out to God and prayed for Him to fill me up so I could pour out. I didn't know if I had any more to give.

When I saw the puppy on Facebook, I absolutely knew better. I did NOT need one more living being to care for in that season. The kids had been with us for three years by that point, but the level of care was still constant. Rewarding, but intense.

No. A puppy would not be a good plan. We already had three dogs in the home. One we'd had before the children came home, a grumpy old man without much tolerance for people. Another belonged to my aging mother, who lived on the bottom level of our home. And our golden retriever was a Christmas gift for all the kids several years earlier. We did not need any more chaos.

But I was drawn. Every time I went to Facebook, pics of the pups drew me in. One in particular, a fluffy white ball of cuteness, called to my very soul. It felt like God was actually nudging me toward this puppy, but could that be? Puppies were messy and a lot of work. Surely God didn't intend . . .

I couldn't shake it. I reached out to the owner, a friend of mine, and the one I liked was available. I went over for a visit and my heart melted into a puddle. Half shepherd, quarter husky, quarter chow, he was soft and fluffy, with big brown eyes. I'd had enough dogs to know that puppies are purposefully adorable to suck you into their vortex before they destroy all the furniture, but still . . . I couldn't resist. I asked my friend to put him on hold for me, and talked to my husband, who graciously chose not to try to talk me out of it—although the slight lift of his eyebrows showed his concern.

> The LORD is my shepherd, I lack nothing. He makes me lie down in green pastures, he leads me beside quiet waters, he refreshes my soul.
>
> —PSALM 23:1–3 (NIV)

The kids had been asking for another dog, and we'd said no many times, so we weren't quite sure how to pull off Mommy getting one. Christmas wasn't too far away. A plan was hatched. My adult daughter would go get the puppy on Christmas morning and bring it home as a gift from my friend. To keep us honest, my friend actually decided to give the pup to us at no cost. How could we possibly refuse such generosity?

Christmas morning came and all the gifts had been distributed. With happy hearts, we rested from all the excitement. And in walked my girl. With my pup.

Even though I knew he was coming, I cried like a baby. I wrapped him up into my arms and cried into his fur. He nuzzled my face, his warm puppy breath warm against my cheek. The kids were all jealous. "Mom's got a dog? Can we share him?"

"Nope," said my sweet man, who had seen how much this meant to me. "This is Mom's dog. You can hold him and love him, but she is his owner. He belongs to her."

He belonged to me.

And he loved me.

God used the puppy, who I named Koda, in my mama world from the very beginning. His training denied logic in its simplicity. Shepherds, huskies and chows are all known for their chewing prowess. But not Koda. We lost not a single shoe to slobbery puppy teeth, not a single piece of carpet to tearing puppy canines. He was potty trained within a week and spent the night in a crate beside my bed, sleeping through until morning in no time at all. He followed me everywhere, toddling behind me wherever I went. The kids would try to distract him, but he was undeterred. Wherever I was, he wanted to be. Even today, as a fully grown 100-pound dog, he follows me into the bathroom, wedging his big body between my legs and the wall. Just to be close.

A few weeks ago, I was utterly spent after walking one of my children through an epic trauma meltdown. Koda was right there. He leaned into my legs and pressed his weight in close. I buried my hands in his fur and bent to rest my face on his massive head. He held it unmoving, carrying the weight of my weariness with his protective stance. When I was on my knees the following morning, calling out to my God for help for the day, Koda was there as well. His body tucked in close, his brown eyes watching me carefully. He sensed when the tears came and leaned in even closer, a single lick wiping the tear away.

Recently I was reading Psalm 23, about how my shepherd leads me besides still waters. As trauma mama to four adopted littles, I need that. I need still waters and I need my Savior, my shepherd. My God knew that, and gave me a puppy shepherd to illustrate his care. When my shepherd follows me with his gaze and leans in close, I'm reminded that my God is as close as my breath. When Koda guards my steps and takes a protective stance, my heart is encouraged that God leads, protects, guides, and sees me through the heartache of this mama life.

> **He tends his flock like a shepherd: He gathers the lambs in his arms and carries them close to his heart; he gently leads those that have young.**
>
> —ISAIAH 40:11

Koda is a steady reminder of God's love and presence. I have had to work so hard to build attachment with my beautiful trauma-scarred babies, pouring out love for years on end. But not with Koda. God gave him to me and Koda attached simply and quickly. Koda loves me unwaveringly. He loves me when I have nothing to give. He loves me whether I'm a great mama or a lousy one. He loves me the way Jesus loves me. And he fills my empty bucket with puppy love.

Which only helps me pour out more.

Ah, my Koda bear.

Angel in a Winter Storm
Leone F. Byron

November 20, 2000, was a day I'll never forget. An early winter storm struck Buffalo during the afternoon. The city was being hit hard, and by late afternoon my managers decided to close the office early and send us home. I gathered my things and headed to my car, only to find it buried under the snow. Thankfully, one of the senior managers helped me to dig it out, and before long, I was headed for home.

I abandoned my normal highway route in favor of the local roads, reasoning that I had a better chance of getting help if I got stuck on a side street. I didn't realize until later just how critical that decision would be.

Snow continued to fall as I drove. Listening to the radio, I heard that schools and businesses all over the city had already emptied out. Everyone was trying to get home, and the traffic, combined with the accumulating snow, made the streets virtually impassable. As darkness descended, I crawled behind a line of cars; it was the world's biggest game of follow the leader. The wet, heavy snow was coming down faster than my wipers could keep up. At times, the cars would stop altogether, and I would use the opportunity to get out and clean out the snow-clogged windshield wipers. The wind and the snow buffeted me, freezing my legs in the skirt I had decided to wear that day.

I turned onto yet another side street and came to a dead stop behind a line of cars. With more cars lined up behind me and snow piled up on both sides, there was nowhere to go. I was stuck. Cold and tired, with nothing to do but sit, I quickly lost my patience. I yelled at the cars in front of me; they weren't moving, and I couldn't understand why. The only break came when someone knocked on my window, offering the last of several large, hot teas that he had been bringing to stranded travelers. Grateful, I thanked him, took the tea, and shut my window against the storm. As the time stretched out and nobody moved, I started to wonder if the people in front of me had abandoned their cars. How long would I be stuck here? I didn't know what else to do but wait.

Finally, I thought I heard a car start. Getting out to investigate, I saw a woman and a child shoveling at the head of the street. Seeing me get out, she sent her child to meet me with the cordless phone she'd brought outside. As I walked toward her, I glanced around and was surprised to see people in the cars I thought had been abandoned.

Reaching the woman and her daughter, I took the phone and called my roommate to let her know I was all right. My roommate breathed a sigh of relief as she told me she had been checking on people and had heard from everyone except me. I hung up the phone and returned it to the woman. She

> "For I was hungry, and you gave Me food; I was thirsty, and you gave Me drink; I was a stranger, and you took Me in."
>
> —MATTHEW 25:35 (NKJV)

introduced herself as Martha and told me that she was a Buffalo police officer. She pointed to her house and invited me to go inside and help myself to whatever I needed.

Grateful for her help, I thanked her and ran into the house. The warmth made me realize how cold I had gotten in the storm. A few minutes later, the other people, four women and three men, joined me. Martha and her daughter came in from shoveling and began making hot coffee and food for everyone.

We talked about the storm as we ate. Almost 30 inches of snow had fallen since early afternoon, and the highways were giant parking lots, with hundreds of people stuck in their cars. A school bus had tipped over on a side street, and while thankfully nobody was hurt, there were schoolchildren who hadn't been able to make it home. I later found out that a neighbor had taken in the stranded children and fed them until they could be reunited with their parents. On the street where we were stranded, it turned out the woman owning the car at the front of the line had abandoned her vehicle, apparently not considering how that would impact the people behind her. Dave, the owner of the truck behind her car, had gone to look for her. He checked the fast-food restaurant two blocks away. While he didn't find her, he decided to bring hot tea for the rest of us. Martha commented that she saw the line of cars when she came out and had assumed that they were abandoned. When

> **For I, the LORD your GOD, will hold your right hand, saying to you, "Fear not, I will help you."**
>
> —ISAIAH 41:13 (NKJV)

GOD'S GIFT OF TOUCH
— Terrie Todd —

IS ANYTHING MORE inviting or comforting at the end of a long day, especially in cold weather, than crawling between soft, warm flannel sheets in one's own bed? God's children can imagine this experience as climbing into their Heavenly Father's lap and being lovingly snuggled in safety and security while they sleep. Every 24 hours, we can feel that flannel and be reminded of God's warmth, presence, acceptance, and love. "In peace I will lie down and sleep, for you alone, Lord, make me dwell in safety" (Psalm 4:8, NIV).

---

she saw me and others who were stranded in our cars, she was happy to help in any way that was possible. Since it seemed that we weren't going anywhere that night, she offered to let us stay with her.

I looked about the house, grateful for Dave's thoughtfulness, and for Martha's kindness. It was a reminder that God, through His leading me onto the side streets and to an angel named Martha, was always looking out for me.

It had gotten late while we talked, and our hostess showed us upstairs. Somehow, she managed to find blankets for everyone. She led us into her front room, where I found a recliner and, exhausted, quickly fell asleep, curled up under a blanket.

The next morning, a few of us made breakfast with Martha while the others went outside to start shoveling. We took turns shoveling, and by noon, Dave said he could get around the car at the front of the line, still abandoned since last night. Hearing this, Martha looked disappointed, saying she was just getting ready to make us lunch.

Finally, it was my turn to go. I hugged Martha and thanked her again for her incredible generosity in taking in eight strangers caught in a storm.

When I made it home shortly afterward, I called friends and family and told them about the angel God had sent to help me and the others who were stuck. Though the journey was exhausting, I had learned some valuable truths about God's presence and provision in the storms of my life.

Midair Meeting
Angela J. Kaufman

I really don't want to talk to anybody this morning, God.

Loaded down with my backpack, small coat, and water bottle, I struggle to walk through the aisle to our seats on the airplane. My husband and I have been awake since 3:00 a.m., and I am already exhausted before we begin the first leg of our trip. The interruption of my sleep hygiene leaves me feeling weak, a bit nauseous, and irritable. Discovering that our seat is in a row near the back of the plane makes me extra weary.

Just what I don't need.

It is going to be a noisy and bumpy ride, and I wonder how I will endure another flight after our layover. Looking ahead, I see that my seat is in the middle of the row, which seals my simmering mood.

As we settle in, I do the cursory nod and hello to the young man looking out the window. I try to stay in my space and mind my own business, but I sense there is an incredible urgency to his demeanor, a lot of anxious energy.

Takeoff makes me nervous, and so I do what I always do in these situations—pray a portion of the Prayer of Saint Patrick: "Christ with me, Christ before me, Christ behind me, Christ in me, Christ beneath me, Christ above me, Christ on my right, Christ on my left, Christ when I lie down, Christ when I sit down . . ." I repeat lines in no particular order, sometimes adding my own phrases, like "Christ be around me," as I envision God's spirit encompassing the outside of the entire plane.

I surrender my discomfort of wanting to avoid people—not yet conscious of receiving a nudge from God—and begin the typical conversation with my seatmate. "Where are you going to today?"

The words tumble out. He tells me that he has almost 24 hours of air travel ahead of him. He had only a small window of time to make it back to Jerusalem for the funeral of a dear family member, and, due to the short notice, his flights are quite bizarre, with layovers in multiple countries. I forget my personal misery and consider what is ahead for him. The disorientation he will be experiencing is overwhelming to us both. Never mind the fact that he is in the early stages of deep grief.

I realize as he is speaking that I had been judging him, initially avoiding the conversation not just because I was tired, but because of the differences in our background.

Oh God, I am ashamed.

Our country recently experienced a violent attack, so common for most countries in the world. The media has plastered faces with different skin tones than mine as conspirators. Yet, I have always maintained a gentle acceptance of those different

> **Hear my prayer, LORD, listen to my cry for help; do not be deaf to my weeping. I dwell with you as a foreigner, a stranger, as all my ancestors were.**
>
> —PSALM 39:12 (NIV)

than me. My feelings had succumbed to a fear that is not of God, and I had almost missed the chance to offer what comfort I can.

Please give me the words, God.

I gently nudge him to talk about his family and the joy he anticipates by seeing them in spite of the circumstances. As the conversation continues, he reveals more details. It is his grandmother who passed, and the loss hit him hard. We converse about the traditions that are part of his heritage when people mourn their family members. His raw emotion sometimes has us both in tears.

> **Consequently, you are no longer foreigners and strangers, but fellow citizens with God's people and also members of his household.**
>
> —EPHESIANS 2:19 (NIV)

I feel God's spirit in me recognize God in his life. Though I am never sure of his religious affiliation, I feel a profound spiritual connection as we talk about the ways in which his family will honor his grandmother, the biblical truths that promise a life with God beyond this world. As the exchange continues, I realize how much we have in common despite all our differences.

What a gift, God!

I feel that we are a brother and sister in our faith. We are fellow pilgrims in our walk with God. Even though we may look different, worship differently, and come from different countries, we are tied together as the family of God.

We continue our dialogue throughout the entire flight, waiting in silence only as the aircraft begins landing procedures.

As we stand, ready to deplane, I assure him of my prayers for the rest of his journey, wishing him safety and smooth connections. He appears to have more strength and less desperation as we part, turning back once more as we wave goodbye and head to our respective gates.

My husband and I hurry to our next connection. I am torn with both a great heaviness of heart for this young man, and a tremendous urge to stop—just stop—and process what has happened. There is no time, and I give my husband the short version of our discussion. I feel grateful that I was able to be there for this young stranger, to give him a chance to talk and do some processing of his own during a long and difficult journey. But while my husband and I wait to board again, it occurs to me that this sad soul was placed in our row as a way for me to sense God's presence. Our meeting was not just for him, it was also for me—to see the bigger picture God was trying to show me, that God is always around me and with me, in every instance. God used each of us to help the other.

This is a holy moment and a holy place.

God draws us closer on our spiritual paths, bringing people into our lives who show us a God we might not expect—a God who helps us look past our immediate circumstances and connects people, a God who shows us how we can be a blessing to one another.

It's amazing what miracles
and little angels and
pure love around you
can bring out.

—Tionne Watkins

CHAPTER 5
Miracle Moments

Miracle on the Bridge.........................150
   Valorie Bridges Fant
Perky's Hummingbird........................155
   Rhoda Blecker
How Wood We Get Back?....................159
   Lisa Livezey
He Hears Our Cries..........................163
   Elsa Kok Colopy
Back Road Miracle...........................168
   Ana Arreola Moore

Miracle on the Bridge
Valorie Bridges Fant

In the autumn of 1976, I made a conscious choice to dedicate my life to the Lord. Shortly afterward, I started attending a church called the Stream in the Desert.

The Stream in the Desert was a coffeehouse ministry. The building, which stood on a busy main street, was a simple two-story brick structure that lacked any ornate features. The front windows were covered in murals, leaving only narrow glimpses inside. Facing the parking lot, painted on an exterior wall, was a large hand that resembled the American flag. The index finger pointed upward to a phrase written in bold, white letters: "One Way Jesus."

I first attended the church during a Wednesday night prayer meeting. Not knowing what to expect, I was uneasy and apprehensive. The moment I entered the front door, I was standing in a cozy, dimly lit room. Brown metal folding chairs lined the unvarnished wooden floors. In every corner, I saw groups of cheerful people gathered together, engaged in lively conversations. Suddenly, the lights turned on, and the crowd took their seats. I spotted an empty chair by the wall and eagerly sat down.

A motley crew of individuals walked in from behind a curtain carrying acoustic guitars and tambourines. In the center of the room, they all sat down in a circle of chairs and started playing music. I watched in curiosity as the people sang the most beautiful songs. With closed eyes and outstretched hands, every person appeared to be standing in the very presence of God. Never had I experienced something so unique and powerful.

When the music finally stopped, a man with a boyish appearance stood up to welcome everyone. He then asked, "Would anyone like to share?" One by one, people stood and shared animated stories of how God had helped them during the week.

As I heard the various testimonies, my heart started to race. My eyes fluttered, and I could feel my entire body tense as if it were struggling to contain a powerful force within me. I felt a persistent inner nudge encouraging me to get up, but fear held me back. I had never spoken in front of a crowd of people before. My heart was beating so fast I could hardly breathe. The next thing I knew, I was springing up from my chair.

> **But God sent me ahead of you . . . to save your lives by a great deliverance.**
>
> —GENESIS 45:7 (NIV)

The entire room strangely went silent, as if the people were telling me, "This is your moment." I stood center stage, with everyone's eyes fixed on me. Then I heard these words coming out of my mouth, "Hi . . . my name is Valorie . . ." From there, everything that had happened to bring me to that appointed time poured out like water. I rambled on for what seemed like hours, and when I finally stopped, the room exploded with cheers. God had led me to this strange and miraculous church, filled with a deliciously diverse group of people. Individuals who were walking with God in the purest form, simply seeking His guidance and presence.

After that Wednesday night prayer meeting, I spent every available moment at the Stream in the Desert, despite the nearly hour-long drive it took for me to get there. With a deep thirst in my soul, I eagerly sought to drink from the river of the water of life.

One cold wintry Sunday morning, after an ice storm had blanketed my small town, I jumped into my car to go to church. I was notorious for not wearing a seat belt, but when I turned on the engine, I heard a quiet voice urging me to put it on today. I foolishly dismissed it.

It was already 9:30 and the service typically started at around 10 o'clock. If I wanted to make it to church on time, I had to step on the gas. In a state of panic, I raced down the driveway to avoid being late. The sun had come out, but the roads were still partially covered with sheets of black ice. I should have been more careful, but my only thought that morning was, *I can't be late!*

As I sped down the open road, I was traveling around 70 miles per hour, rapidly approaching the bridge passing over the highway. Without warning, I saw an enormous stretch of shimmering ice that covered the entire road in front of me. On the opposite side of the road, I saw a large tractor trailer. As it got closer to the westbound onramp for the highway, it started to slow down.

Once again, I heard the quiet voice say to me, "The truck is going to turn in front of you."

As the voice foretold, the truck immediately began to turn. It was clear the driver was unaware of my silver Sunbird barreling down the road.

My initial instinct was to slam on the brakes. But being a Michigan driver, I knew that if I tried to brake on the slippery ice, I would completely lose control of my car. My mind raced in a million different directions, desperately seeking a solution. A terrifying thought screamed through my mind: *You're not wearing your seat belt!* But it was too late!

It was all happening so quickly, and yet the truck appeared to be turning in slow motion. I watched the trailer getting closer and closer, like a giant, flashing billboard, but there was no way I could safely stop. In that somber moment, I knew this was it. My life was coming to a horrible end. I gripped the steering wheel tightly and cried, "Oh, God!" Then I closed my eyes and prepared for the impact.

It's difficult to describe what happened next. It was as if I disappeared for a brief moment, lost somewhere in a timeless void. The only thing I am certain of is that I was not present at that instant.

> **Then the angel showed me the river of the water of life, as clear as crystal, flowing from the throne of God and of the Lamb.**
>
> —REVELATION 22:1 (NIV)

When I became aware of my surroundings again, I discovered that my car was parked on the right-hand shoulder of the bridge, with a view of the traffic below. The engine was stopped. I sat there, dazed, trying to figure out what had happened.

When I looked into my rearview mirror, much to my astonishment, I saw the very same tractor trailer still in the process of turning onto the on-ramp. From the window of the cab, I could see a burly-looking man staring back at me. I'm not

GOD'S GIFT OF SIGHT
— Terrie Todd —

WALKING THROUGH A garden with the vivid reds, oranges, and yellows of nasturtiums or the pinks and purples of petunias, it's difficult to imagine a more glorious use of color. Yet people who've had near-death experiences frequently report seeing vibrant colors for which we have no words because they don't exist in our world. God's creativity knows no bounds. All that we see now is merely a glimpse of what awaits us in eternity: "'What no eye has seen, what no ear has heard, and what no human mind has conceived'— the things God has prepared for those who love him—these are the things God has revealed to us by his Spirit" (1 Corinthians 2:9, NIV).

---

sure what he had seen, but the confused look on his face made me think he may have witnessed something unexplainable too.

In the realm of natural occurrences, I am at a loss as to why I didn't crash my car into the side of the truck. I found myself on the other side of the truck, without a scratch, parked with the engine off. However, in the realm of the supernatural, I believe that when I cried, "Oh God!" His ministering angels miraculously lifted my car, and safely set it down on the shoulder of the bridge.

Psalm 91:11–12 (NIV) says, "For he will command his angels concerning you to guard you in all your ways; they will lift you up in their hands, so that you will not strike your foot against a stone." However, on this day, it happened to be a tractor trailer! Nothing can compare to the wonder of God's miracles.

Perky's Hummingbird
Rhoda Blecker

Karen, our dog trainer, told my husband, Keith, and me in no uncertain terms, "If you have two dogs, you have a pair of dogs. If you have three dogs, you have a pack. And if you don't understand pack dynamics, bad things can happen." Unfortunately, she was a lot better at training dogs than she was at training us, but we didn't need to deal with those mysterious "pack dynamics" until we had increased our canine family to four.

We didn't set out to rescue that many dogs, but we were suckers when a dog wandered into the cul de sac on which we lived. We always waited to see if anyone else in the area would adopt the dog; if no one did, we stepped up. That was how we ended up with three female dogs, and one dominant male, who made sure everyone knew that he was the alpha in the pack. Elijah was a Doberman/husky mix who got his name when we opened the door for the prophet Elijah at the end of our Passover Seder, and the dog walked right in, as if he had been waiting on the front porch.

After three years of successful pack life, Elijah suddenly died. We had no idea what his absence would mean to our remaining three dogs, Perky, Spunky, and Jessif. While Spunky had no desire to be alpha, both Perky and Jessif thought they should take over the position. That resulted in a dogfight in our living room from which Perky emerged with a long, deep slash across her chest. We rushed her to the vet for stitches and isolated her to heal, but hoped we could bring our three girls together again. We consulted Karen, and that was how we learned the phrase "insecure alpha."

"Perky thinks she is the one who needs to take over as pack leader now," Karen said, "but she isn't confident enough, so she's being too aggressive to compensate. Once trust is lost, it almost never comes back. You will have to keep her isolated, or there will be more fights."

> **There are companions to keep one company, and there is a friend more devoted than a brother.**
>
> —PROVERBS 18:24 (JPS)

That news was heartbreaking. Friends asked us why we didn't just find another home for her, but that wasn't an option. Perky loved us, and we had promised her a forever home. So we set up my office as her new home-within-a-home. When Spunky and Jessif were loose in the rest of the house, she had to stay in the office; when she was with us, the other two were shut in the master bedroom. I spent as much time with her as I could, but she was alone so much that I felt sad and guilty. I prayed that she would adjust to eating her meals and sleeping apart from the rest of us.

The office began to take on Perky's not-unpleasant doggy smell, and both Keith and I became used to hearing her distinctive, joyous bark when she was reunited with us. She greeted me with it when I entered the office, then usually settled down in her bed and sighed contentedly while I worked. Every time I had to leave her, I hoped she was getting used to the way we had to live now. I didn't stop brooding about it, however, until the day I met Perky's hummingbird.

I was at my desk one afternoon about six months after the dogfight, when we had settled into the routine of a Perky-separate life that dulled but did not banish my guilt. Perky suddenly leaped out of her bed and trotted to one of the open office windows. The sill was low enough that she could put her front paws on it while still sitting on the floor. Her nose almost touched the screen as she leaned forward. I smiled at her and was turning back to my work when I saw a flash of motion on the other side of the screen and looked more closely. It was a hummingbird, which came to a sudden stop with its beak directly in front of the dog's nose and hovered there.

> **I, I am He who comforts you!**
>
> —ISAIAH 51:12 (JPS)

I expected Perky to bark at the bright green bird, but she did not. The two of them seemed to spend at least a minute in silent communion with each other. I fancied that this was not their first meeting, but that this sort of thing happened often. Perky had, I thought, made a friend. That alleviated a lot of my worry for her, even if, I told myself, I was imagining how important it might be to her.

About eight months later, Perky's spleen burst. We took her to the vet and made the difficult choice to let her go. As the vet administered the shot, I cuddled Perky and told her she was safe and loved.

We waited a couple of days before taking out of the office her bed, her food dish, and the weasel toy she had treasured. We hired a company to clean the rugs, and soon the particular smell that reminded us of her was gone. I could work with the office door open, and the other dogs could wander in and out if they wanted.

But every so often, when Keith and I were in the living room, I would think I heard Perky bark. I would look up, startled, to see Keith also looking around. He asked me, "Did you hear that?" It happened a few more times over the next week or so, each time startling and unnerving us.

One day, I was working in the office when I suddenly smelled Perky again, as clearly as if she were still there. I quickly glanced around the room. Nothing had changed. Then I saw it. At the window, the hummingbird hovered, in exactly the spot where I had first seen it, its beak almost touching the screen. The bird stayed in place, its wings moving too fast to be seen, for what seemed like a very long time. Then it darted away, and the Perky smell was gone.

Keith and I never heard her bark again, but I knew I hadn't imagined it. Perky had stayed around until she had the opportunity to say goodbye to her friend, and then she was free to move on. I sometimes pray now that I will be given such a beautiful and loving departure.

How Wood We Get Back?
Lisa Livezey

"C'mon, Mom, let's take the road that cuts through the woods!" my 13-year-old son Trevor insisted repeatedly as we drove back from town on familiar country backroads. We frequented these parts, deep in the Maine woods, for two weeks every summer, staying at a rustic family cabin we affectionately called "Camp." Trevor had noticed a logging road on our car's GPS that extended from the road we were traveling to Pond Road, which led to Camp.

Years back, paper companies owned large tracts of Maine, and the logging roads they forged still crisscross throughout the state's pine forests. These rough-cut, stony roads now are used mostly by folks having fun on snowmobiles and ATVs.

Trevor continued his pleading, but I hesitated. My car was older and the GPS software a bit outdated. Most likely the road he saw would be intact, but why take a chance?

"Let's try it, Mom!" Trevor persisted.

I wavered, then yielded to his whim.

Reluctantly, I turned off the paved road and started north on the bumpy logging road, following the car's GPS. A quarter-mile down was a left turn, and then another turn, after which we reached a road that should have connected to Pond Road. It was straight but steep. We began going down, down, down the hill with our car rattling and bumping over sizable uneven stones. *My tires aren't made for this,* I stewed. *This road had better go through, because I don't think my car will get back up that steep incline.* I thought about my husband relaxing back at Camp and imagined calling him with the news that our car was stuck deep in the woods needing to be towed. Not a happy thought.

We reached the valley floor and the road continued up, up, up to the next rise. At the crest of the hill, we stopped and got out of the car. From here, the road fell off steeply, continuing down hundreds of feet, disappearing, and becoming visible again on the next ridge. There was no way our car could do it. You'd need some kind of off-road vehicle. "We have to go back," I said.

> **You provide a broad path for my feet, so that my ankles do not give way.**
>
> —2 SAMUEL 22:37 (NIV)

"You drive back—I'll hike this road back to Camp," Trevor insisted, excited at the thought of exploring unknown territory. I hesitated again. Based on the GPS, the familiar road lay just beyond that next ridge, maybe about a mile. Trevor was big for his age, strong, and fit. *It would be an easy hike for him,* I thought, *and teenage boys need wholesome outlets for adventure.* My experience with these logging roads was that they eventually connected to civilization, and I felt sure this one would lead Trevor in the right direction.

I thought about giving Trevor my phone, but then I thought about how dangerously rocky and steep the road to this point had been. What if I got stuck? I could be walking for miles, hoping to find a random stranger to call my husband. I opted to keep my phone, trusting in the car's GPS along with Trevor's youth, vigor, and proven resourcefulness. He was accustomed to the forests around Camp, and there seemed no reason to worry.

We parted ways and Trevor bounded off down the trail like a deer. I tentatively turned the car around, heading slowly back down, down, down, reaching the valley floor and beginning back up, up, up. My car began to struggle.

"Please, Jesus, please help me get back to the main road!!! Please, Jesus, please!!!" I called out desperately over and over.

There is no explanation for what happened next. I can only tell you that a split second later, I found myself sitting in the driver's seat, hands on the wheel, in a completely different place. In front of me was the paved road. My car was back where we had started!

> ## So he returned home to his father.
>
> —LUKE 15:20 (NLT)

Relief flooded me, then gratitude, then wonder. *How did my car get here? Did I zone out while driving?* I was sure I had never finished that steep incline or made either of the two turns. Had my car somehow been picked up by divine hands and placed at its starting point?

Whatever just happened, I'll take it! I sighed in relief and thanked the Lord again out loud.

Returning to Camp, I found my husband happily fishing off the dock but there was no sign of Trevor. *He'll be back momentarily,* I thought. My husband was worried, though. I could tell he questioned my decision to send Trevor off alone. "There are bears in the woods," he said.

We were preparing to go search for Trevor when we heard a rumbling sound coming down the pine-needled driveway. An old motorcycle came into view with a gray-bearded, flannel-shirt-wearing mountain man at the handlebars. Sitting behind him, holding on tightly, was Trevor!

The motorcycle halted before us, sputtering to a stop. Trevor, with jeans muddied to the knee, climbed off. The mountain man disembarked, removed his helmet with gnarled hands, and introduced himself. His last name was familiar and I recalled seeing it when driving to town—white painted letters on a red mailbox alongside a dirt driveway that disappeared into the woods.

We enjoyed a few minutes chatting with this Mainer about his 100 wooded acres, which he selectively harvested and replanted with quality hardwood.

Trevor confessed to having ventured off the logging road in search of a shortcut. He'd begun sinking to his knees in marshy grasses, eventually reaching a clearing where the mountain man's cabin stood. Knowing we'd be worried, Trevor knocked on the door in hopes of calling us. He later described how his new friend, upon answering the door, said, "Well, where'd you come from?" A thick, tattered phone book was produced and vintage wall phone offered for Trevor's use, but then the mountain man offered him a ride back to Camp.

Not only had God's angels lifted my car and placed it at the paved road, but he'd simultaneously provided a human angel to give Trevor a lift! The Maine thing for which I was most thankful—we'd both arrived safely back at Camp.

He Hears Our Cries
Elsa Kok Colopy

The sky outside my window was pitch black when I jolted awake. I reached for my phone, and the bright numbers on the screen told me it was 1:42 a.m.

Wilna, I suddenly thought. Our daughter had called when she left her friend's house, as per our normal routine. We didn't expect her home until 2, but some type of motherly instinct had woken me early.

I opened the Life360 app and clicked on Wilna's name. The dot representing her drive home blinked at an intersection just a few miles away. It blinked again. One minute later it blinked again. It was oddly placed as well—just to the right of the intersection instead of in the middle of it. Something was wrong.

I called my husband, who was downstairs waiting to make sure Wilna arrived safely and to welcome her home. At 19, she was able to stay out later on weekends, but we still wanted to make sure she made it home safely. He answered my call from the couch downstairs. "Her dot's not moving," I said, my heart beginning to race. "I think something is wrong."

"I'll call her," Brian said.

He called. I called. No answer.

"I'll head over that way," he said.

I checked the phone to see if the car was still in the same spot. It was.

Brian left the house, but before he reached the main road, he called me. "I just saw a sheriff turn down our road," he said. "I think he's coming to our house."

He stayed on the phone with me as I went downstairs to the front door. The doorbell rang as Brian was cresting the hill that would put him in view of the intersection. "I see lights," he said. "It doesn't look good."

I opened our front door to see the sheriff standing there. He looked somber and I could feel my whole body begin to shake with adrenaline. "Are you the parent of Wilna Colopy?" he asked. I nodded.

"She's been in an accident," he said. "The accident looks bad, but she is alive. She isn't conscious, but her vitals seem steady. She is in the ambulance on the way to the hospital. Would you like me to take you there?"

"Yes, please," I said. I took a deep, shaking breath, trying to steady myself. Brian was still on the phone with me and heard the news as well. I relayed the hospital info to him and told him I'd meet him there. "Let me just tell my mother," I added. "She lives downstairs and we have other kids in the home."

I ran downstairs and my words came out in a rush as I woke my mom from a deep slumber. She immediately began praying as I dashed back upstairs and out the front door to accompany the sheriff. As we drove out of the neighborhood, he explained, "I'll have to transfer you to another officer once we get to the accident site and she will take you the rest of the way. Now, just know, the accident looks very bad. Try not to focus on the car, OK?"

When we arrived at the intersection, though, I couldn't help but focus on the car. It looked like half the car it once was, the front end literally wrapped around a large pole. Apparently she had fallen asleep and had run into the pole at nearly 60 mph.

From my vantage point, it didn't seem like anyone could have survived that kind of crash. Or if survival were possible, the injuries would be significant. I forced myself to breathe in and breathe out, knowing that this was one of those life-changing moments I would never forget. *Lord, have mercy*, I whispered over and over to my God.

The drive to the nearest trauma hospital was still 30 minutes away. The back seat of the police cruiser was hard and cool, void of any comforts; it was meant for transporting criminals, not terrified mothers. We pulled into the ER parking area and the officer kindly escorted me inside. There I reunited with Brian, both of us without words as we leaned into each other.

When the nurse finally ushered us in to see our daughter, I was shocked by how unharmed she seemed. Wilna had a brace around her neck, and an IV in her arm, but otherwise she looked as if she were soundly sleeping,

"We believe she has a significant concussion," the doctor told us, "but she has no broken bones and our initial evaluation shows no internal injuries either. It's truly a miracle."

I looked at our girl. The windshield had shattered, but there was barely a scratch on her. The dash had moved up under the steering wheel and she had no broken bones. While she often

> **For he will command his angels concerning you to guard you in all your ways; they will lift you up in their hands, so that you will not strike your foot against a stone.**
>
> —PSALM 91:11–12 (NIV)

GOD'S GIFT OF SMELL
— Kim Taylor Henry —

WE TEND TO take noses for granted, but they are truly one of God's little miracles. Who could ever have imagined that two little holes in a skin-and-cartilage tent above the mouth could provide such calm, such pleasure—and such disgust and clear warning against things that could harm?

God, in His unsurpassable ingenuity, fashioned a small addition to our face that can provide both delight and protection. Try taking time to pause in your daily routine today and just inhale. What do you smell? What are the scents of your world, and what is God telling you through them?

---

complained about being a tiny thing, her small stature had ultimately saved her.

The days after the accident were a blur of doctors, hospital rooms, and sleepless nights. The final diagnosis was a severe concussion and a torn PCL from the hard hit to her knee. She would require physical therapy, but no surgery. Wilna was going to be OK.

One quiet morning, I sat at the table with my journal and paged back to the day of the accident. I'd been praying for our girl and wanted to read what I'd written. I gasped out loud as I read my closing paragraph from November 4, just hours before the wreck. "It is a fight and I will keep fighting. There is beauty and life ahead for this child, Lord. Pave the way, strengthen her frame, save her life." I read the words again. "Strengthen her frame. Save her life." *Strengthen her frame*—she had no broken bones. *Save her life*—she had survived. I had written those words the very day of her accident, before it even happened. Goosebumps ran up and down my arms.

Later that afternoon, my husband and I visited the car and took pictures of the damage. We gathered up her personal belongings, including her set of keys. Again, my breath caught as I read the small silver keychain attached to her keys: "For he will order his angels to protect you wherever you go."

Save her life.
For he will order his angels to protect you.
Prayers spoken before the crash.
Prayers answered during the crash.
No other explanation but divine intervention.
Thank You, Jesus.

Back Road Miracle
Ana Arreola Moore

Everyone said that the summer of 1980 was the hottest summer ever recorded in the state of Texas—and that's exactly where I found myself!

I had been approved to go on a mission trip abroad and begin a teaching position at a Christian school in San Jose, Costa Rica. There was a tender spot in my heart for Costa Rica. I loved the people, the mountains, and the language. There were a lot of preparations to be made, and I needed a break, so I decided to take a two-week vacation to visit my sister and her husband in Fort Worth, Texas, and then take a side trip into Louisiana to visit a friend.

The blast of hot air hit my Michigan skin like an oven as I traveled to visit with my friend Marilyn in Leesville, Louisiana. I'd left early in the morning to try to avoid the worst of the heat, but it was hours past that time now. My sister had been worried as I said goodbye, and she insisted I get the car insurance for the rental car. Later, she told me that she just had a *feeling* about this trip I was taking alone.

We had a wonderful time visiting and eating some of that great Louisiana food. Too soon it was time for me to leave. "I sure needed this break," I told my friend as I said my goodbyes and thank-yous.

I headed off early, because it was a six-hour drive back to my sister's place, and I didn't want to travel at night. In order to get to the main highway, I had to travel down some country roads. As I left town, I passed a huge sign with a wrecked car next to it warning drivers to drive safely. Later, I would look back on it and think about how ironic it was.

It was a very hot, humid day, but I was enjoying the ride. Suddenly a car coming toward me made a turn in front of me. I slammed on the brakes to avoid hitting them head-on, and I lost control of the car.

The next thing I knew, I was lying in a ditch on my back. I was in such a state of shock that it took me a few minutes to realize I'd been thrown through the windshield of my car. I tried to get up, but I fell back down.

> **The eternal God is your refuge, and underneath are the everlasting arms.**
>
> —DEUTERONOMY 33:27 (NIV)

As soon as they saw I was awake, five or six people surrounded me and told me not to move. I could hear the motor of the rental car somewhere near me. In my confused state, I thought I could get up and keep going to Texas. I had no idea of the extent of my injuries. I had no idea where the people around me had come from.

They formed a circle around me in that grassy, stony ditch. One of them asked, "Can we pray for you?"

Who are these people? I wondered. But no matter who they were, prayer never hurt. I nodded yes to give them permission. They all laid their hands on my bleeding, bruised body and began to pray. I don't remember what they said, but I felt a heightened sense of God's presence, an overwhelming peace and joy.

An ambulance arrived, and first responders assessed my injuries. They found I had a broken jaw, as evidenced by the swelling around the dislocated joint and the blood and glass on my face. I was immediately taken to the local hospital of Leesville, but they didn't have the facilities to do the necessary surgery, so they had to transport me to the nearest city, Shreveport, 50 miles away.

I don't know how they knew to contact my friend Marilyn, but she came to the hospital. All I remember is that she came in, saw me, and then ran out. She told me later that my face was so swollen, and it was such a shock to her, that she threw up in the hallway.

Once at the Shreveport hospital, I was taken to have every part of my body X-rayed. I was now coming out of shock, and intense pain was coursing all through my body. Marilyn kept praying and pacing outside the exam room. Later, she told me God had given her a verse to pray: "The eternal God is your refuge, and underneath are the everlasting arms" (Deuteronomy 33:27, NIV).

My jaw needed surgery, and the procedure was scheduled for the next morning. Thus began a long exhausting night of pain, with Marilyn by my side talking and praying for me.

What a welcome relief the anesthesia was in the morning! As I came to, I could no longer speak, because my mouth was wired shut. The doctors told me I was a walking miracle. After being thrown out of my car while going 55 miles an hour, my injuries could have been much worse. I thought back to the mysterious group who had prayed over me immediately after the accident and gave thanks to God for sending them to bring

His peace—and also His healing—in those critical moments after the accident.

I stayed in the hospital five days, kept company by the joyful presence of my roommate, who was ironically named Miss Paine. When it was time for me to be discharged, my sister and her husband came to bring me back to Texas. The weather was hot and steamy, and I looked a mess with my swollen face and scrapes on my arms and face. For weeks I kept finding embedded glass in my back and legs that had to be removed.

It was decided that I would fly back to Michigan with my father, who had come to bring me home. What a couple my father and I were on that trip! I was not able to speak clearly with my wired jaw, and my father could not speak English at all, only Spanish. God's presence and joy held me up as we traveled home.

Once home, my life as it had been before the accident came to a halt. I needed extensive dental work. I could only ingest nutrition through a straw. I was dependent on others to help me, because I could not drive myself anywhere.

The doctors told me it would take 6 to 8 weeks for my jaw to recover. I was supposed to leave for my teaching job in Costa Rica at a Christian school in August, only a few weeks away. I knew I was not going to be able to go.

> **The LORD is my strength and my shield; my heart trusts in him, and he helps me. My heart leaps for joy, and with my song I praise him.**
>
> —PSALM 28:7 (NIV)

It was at that time that I immersed myself in journaling and praying. I felt a solid peace as I gave my dream of going to Costa Rica to the Lord. I asked Him, "What now?" He began to open other doors for me to walk through.

They say that God shows up "in the midst" of our most difficult times. For me, God showed up throughout the accident and its aftermath, from the angels who surrounded me when I woke up to the nurses and first responders who shared their humor with me throughout the recovery. God's joyful presence carried me then, and it continues to carry me today as He leads me to adventures I could never have imagined.

The dreams which reveal the supernatural are promises and messages that God sends us directly: they are nothing but His angels, His ministering spirits, who usually appear to us when we are in a great predicament.

—Paracelsus

CHAPTER 6
Visions and Messages from God

No Time for Goodbye 176
    Pamela Montgomery

Pursued by God 182
    Marlene Kropf

My Sister's Dance 186
    Robin Ayscue

Not Just Another Day on the Farm 190
    Kathleen Stauffer

An Angel in Dickies 194
    Susan Shumway

The Voice 199
    Alice H. Murray

The Final Gift 203
    Jeannie Hughes

No Time for Goodbye
Pamela Montgomery

When my husband died, there was no warning, no time to say goodbye.

Following a stroke and many surgeries, Ron's health had been bad for 24 years, and the suffering made him miserable inside and out. He knew I was unhappy, too, seeing him in pain and living in misery. We had been married for 49 years, with all the ups and downs that married couples have, but our marriage survived because of our love, commitment, and appreciation for each other. So on that sunny, lovely Sunday morning in early June 2018 when he took his own life, I was devastated. Even though we had both known that his poor health meant he would die sooner rather than later, I was taken completely by surprise, and the grief tore me apart.

My best friend flew in the next day to be with me. She had been a counselor, and together we dissected Ron's decision. We worked on and off for 5 days, turning all the facts we knew and the emotions in our hearts inside out and upside down. Working hard with me, she brought us both to a place of peace and understanding. Of course I missed Ron. I grieved his death and had many ugly cries. But throughout those initial days of loss, I was upheld by God's love and the love and support of friends and family. I felt as if I was healing every day, facing the grief when it washed over me. I was finding myself in a new season of living, and I'd come to a state of peace within my soul. Thankfully, the dear friend who had helped me through Ron's passing stayed in close contact, as did many others.

What happened next, I could never have conceived, anticipated, or wished for. One night, about 2 months after Ron's death, I was sitting in bed, contentedly reading with the light on. All of a sudden, my husband appeared in the door of the bedroom, dressed as he usually was at night, in jeans and bare chested. Ron walked over to the bed and lay with his head in my lap, looking content. When I reached out to touch him, I could feel every hair on his chest, and his skin was as warm and real as it was when he was alive.

Nothing was said. And then, just as suddenly as he appeared, he vanished, leaving nothing but myself and my book. There was nothing frightening in this encounter, just peace, calm acceptance, and a sense of completion.

About two weeks later, Ron appeared again while I was reading in bed. He entered the room and lay down beside me with his back touching me, just as he did when he was alive. And then, like the time before, he vanished without a trace,

> **What are humans that you are mindful of them or mortals that you care for them? You have made them for a little while lower than the angels; you have crowned them with glory and honor, subjecting all things under their feet.**
>
> —HEBREWS 2:6–8 (NRSVUE)

leaving me with a sense of peace and calm. I understood these encounters as an opening from our life beyond this one as reassurance of Ron's love for me.

Thankfully, I had journaled many blessings that were bestowed upon me immediately after his death. As these wonderful visitations continued over time, I kept journaling about them, using that as a method to process what was happening, since I didn't feel comfortable sharing the experiences with others at first. As I reflected on what had happened, I came to the understanding that these were signs of God's love, experiences that He sent to comfort me. I decided to share my story, hoping it might also help comfort others and give them courage to talk about their own experiences.

When he was alive, Ron tried to take a walk every day. His usual route went around the neighborhood and on the sidewalk of a busy boulevard. He was a familiar figure, making his way along with the help of a tall wooden stick, which prompted the neighbor girls to dub him "Moses"!

As he walked, he looked down, not only to keep from tripping but also to look for treasures. He found wallets, credit cards, nuts and bolts, bungie cords, broken jewelry, and money—lots of coins. If he could identify the person who an object belonged to, he returned it. The other pieces he called his "treasures" and kept in a junk jar. He took his time cleaning and sorting the coins, separating the "keepers" from the ones that were so damaged they needed to be recycled, wrapping the two piles up separately so that the bank would know which were which. The tellers loved to see him come in with his finds, and he became a legend among the bank employees.

Shortly after Ron's death, I sorted and bagged up nearly all of his clothes for a men's mission nearby. I know he would be very pleased to see them used by others. For space reasons, his closet and dresser were in our spare bedroom. After moving the clothing out, I made sure this room was totally clean, the closet emptied, and nothing left on the bed or on the floor. A week or two later, I pulled out the vacuum to do some routine cleaning, and I began in that bedroom. Lo and behold, there was a shiny new dime in the exact middle of the open area of the carpet. I had emptied all of Ron's pockets; I had checked that room many times, and it was void of any extra clutter. This had to have been my husband leaving a sign—his signature in the form of a coin!

> **I want their hearts to be encouraged and united in love, so that they may have all the riches of assured understanding and have the knowledge of God's mystery, that is, Christ, in whom are hidden all the treasures of wisdom and knowledge.**
>
> —COLOSSIANS 2:2–3 (NRSVUE)

Months after my Ron died, I decided to visit friends near Baltimore. My friends garnered tickets for a play at the Kennedy Center, and I was looking forward to a nice, fun weekend. When it was time for the three of us to take our seats in the empty row, my friend entered first, followed by me and then her husband. Whoops! I thought perhaps she would rather sit beside her husband, so we traded seats.

Throughout that moving and rustling around, as we settled in, she looked down at the armrest and then pointed, grabbing my attention. There was a shiny new quarter. No other audience members were close enough to have placed it there, and if it had been left over from a previous performance, the cleaners would have seen it and picked it up. And why would anyone have left a quarter right there?

My friend said it: "It's Ron!" There he was again, letting me know he loved me and was continually looking over me.

———◆———

In the fall after Ron's death, while preparing for a trip with my best friend, I began my usual packing routine. I pulled out the empty suitcase and began to assemble the items that I usually travel with. One of them was a bright blue caftan, which I kept on top of a large basket with other necessary items. But when I went to retrieve it, the caftan was not on top, nor underneath, nor near the basket. Where was it?

I looked everywhere I could think of, and then retraced my path over and over in case I'd missed it the first time. I looked in drawers; I looked in the laundry; I looked in the most unlikely places. I kept returning to the basket to look yet again. It was nowhere to be found.

Finally, the caftan still missing, I decided there was nothing left to do but look once again in all those places. Back to the basket and—lo and behold—lying neatly folded on top of the basket was the bright blue caftan! No one had been in my home. I did not need new glasses. I did not think I was that crazy.

Did Ron help me find it? Or did he hide it first and then return it to me, like a hug? All I am sure about is that Ron still loves me and is still with me. I believe he has become my guardian angel.

We read over and over in the holy Scripture that God is with us and will never leave us, that Jesus and the angels are nearer than we think. All of the incidents I described above—and many, many other unexplainable occurrences—I refer to as Holy Spirit moments. Because of these encounters, I am more and more sensitive to feeling God's presence. I've come to believe that they are meant to help me see God anew, to give me peace and comfort, and to make my life exciting!

Pursued by God
Marlene Kropf

When a philosophy class showed up as a course requirement during my third year of college, I was thrilled. At last I would be able to dig deep into ancient and modern habits of thought and explore questions that intrigued and puzzled me.

Raised in a Christian family, I had absorbed a traditional view of God as the Source of all—Creator of heaven and earth and all humankind. I had been nurtured on stories of Jesus and loved the humble Galilean. I experienced the Holy Spirit as my trustworthy guide in daily life. Questions of faith revolved mainly around issues of behavior: What should I do as a follower of Jesus? How should I live my life?

I had little experience with doubt or distrust of Scripture. Everyone around me seemed confident of their beliefs. Yet as a student on a secular college campus, I encountered thinkers and writers who did not share my familiar assumptions about who God is and what God is doing in the world. In fact, some writers scorned the faith of believers, accusing them of superstition and lack of intellectual rigor. Others disputed the relevance of faith and considered it an outmoded worldview no longer necessary or viable in the modern world.

I was shocked at first to read these thoughtful writers and philosophers challenging the existence of God, then intrigued. For the first time, I began to examine my own assumptions about the existence and nature of God and about human beings. Can we prove that God exists? If we can't, does that mean the entire faith tradition in which I had been nurtured was a flimsy web of conjecture? And if God isn't part of the picture, where did we come from? Why are we here? How should we live?

Seeking answers and a path forward, I haunted the college library, especially the philosophy shelves. With only my intellect as a guide, I was soon overwhelmed with questions that seemed to defy resolution. Even on a warm spring day, the air in the library felt cold as I fell deeper and deeper into a dark and unknown place. When I admitted, eventually, that no philosopher could fully prove the existence of God, I felt hopeless. Had I just been fooling myself all along?

I felt like the ground was falling away beneath my feet. My faith was precious to me; it helped me to understand who I was and how to live my life. But if God wasn't real, then how could I justify living as though He was? I would just be living a lie.

> **You hem me in, behind and before, and you lay your hand upon me.**
>
> —PSALM 139:5 (NIV)

Throughout the week that followed, the feeling of heaviness, even hopelessness, persisted. I felt empty, bereft, cut off. It was a grievous loss, as though some bright light had been extinguished. After all, God had always been part of my world. Now I felt alone in the universe.

As the days wore on, however, I became aware of a puzzling phenomenon—a strange sense that I was being followed. At first I brushed off the sensation and tried to ignore it, but when the experience returned, it was so vivid that it cut through my resistance. I could almost feel the hot breath of someone just behind me. The presence stayed with me, returning for several days. I felt sure that if I turned around, I would see someone. It was like the experience described by the psalmist, "You hem me in, behind and before, and lay your hand upon me" (Psalm 139:5, NRSVUE).

By the end of the week, I gave up. As bewildering as the experience was, in the deepest part of myself, I knew that it was God reaching out to me.

"You win!" I conceded. "I know it's You, God. I have no idea what You want from me, but You've certainly made your presence known." I finally had the proof I needed—not in the form of a philosophical argument, but in the reality of God pursuing me. I had forgotten that the heart also teaches and that our everyday experiences are also wondrous sources of revelation. Mind, heart, and body—all are organs of enlightenment. Gradually I would come to see that faith is not only about intellectual assumptions; it is fundamentally a relationship of trust, a whole-person communion and union with One who loves us forever and beyond all telling.

> When you search for me, you will find me; if you seek me with all your heart.
>
> —JEREMIAH 29:13 (NRSVUE)

Years later, when I discovered the writings of Christian mystics, I found companions who honored such direct and unmediated experiences of God's presence. Some of them, like Julian of Norwich and Meister Eckhart, were also brilliant thinkers who plumbed the depths of their experiences and labored

GOD'S GIFT OF HEARING
— Eryn Lynum —

GOD DESIGNED MOST owls with slightly offset ears. With one ear positioned marginally higher than the other, an owl can precisely pinpoint the location of a sound. Their asymmetrical ears enable them to hone in on subtle noises—even a tiny rodent scurrying beneath snow.

While owl ears can detect sounds ten times fainter than a human's ears, God designed people with heightened spiritual hearing. He enables His children to hear His still, small voice amid society's deafening clatter. The more familiar a person becomes with God's voice—the more that they tune their "higher ear" to divine messages—the more adept they'll become in identifying His words from among the many others vying for attention.

---

diligently to communicate their thoughts and experiences, a boon to seekers like me who longed to integrate the intellect with other ways of knowing.

Ever since those days of doubt and unbelief in college, a conviction about God's presence has not left me. Like Jacob who wrestled with an angel, I felt marked by my encounter with God. I was humbled by the divine visitation and continued to ponder its meaning. Today I wait in hope and expectation for more of the mystery to be revealed.

My Sister's Dance
Robin Ayscue

It was time for us to leave again. Each day was getting harder and harder as we watched the life in my sister's body rapidly draining away. Each time we left, we wondered, *How will she be when we return? Will she be able to talk, to respond? Will she even know us?*

My beautiful sister, Beverly, was getting so very close to heaven. She had been diagnosed with pancreatic cancer just under twelve months ago. We had been thankful for each day with her throughout this year of struggle. The doctors had recently released her over to hospice care, knowing they had tried all that they could to give her body an earthly healing. Now, we waited for her heavenly healing. It was not the answer to prayer we had wanted. The answer God gave required us to place our trust in Him and remember that He knew best, no matter how painful it was for us to accept. Soon, my sister's pain would be over forever.

On one particular night, we had all said our goodnights to her. I lingered in her room as I always did when I was visiting, so I would be the last to leave her bedside. I stood at the door to her bedroom and watched her breathe as she drifted to sleep. The room was still and quiet.

Suddenly I saw the most beautiful smile cross her face—she just lit up. Without opening her eyes, she slowly raised her right hand into the air. She began to lean forward as though she was trying to get out of bed. I quietly stepped over to her and took her hand, which was cupped and high in the air by now. She immediately opened her eyes and looked at me, startled.

"That was the weirdest thing," she kept repeating. "That was so weird, I can't believe it."

"What happened?"

"I was dancing. It was so beautiful and slow."

Trying to always lighten her mood, I responded, "We're Baptist. You haven't ever danced a day in your life!"

She smiled and said, "I know. But I was, I really was dancing! It was with the most beautiful man I've ever seen." If you could have seen the glow on her face, you wouldn't question whether or not she was telling the truth. I understood exactly who she had been dancing with.

> **While he was blessing them, he left them and was taken up to heaven.**
>
> —LUKE 24:51 (NIV)

Two nights later, I was sitting beside her bed as she was sleeping. The presidential debate was on her small TV. I had it muted, as what they had to say seemed very unimportant just then. Then two-year-old grandnephew Ben came bouncing into the room and hopped up on my lap. This was extremely unusual. Young as he was, he seemed to sense that something wasn't right, and he had been withdrawing from his Maw-Maw Beverly's room more and more. But here was his sweet little smiling face.

We quietly played with his tiny Barney figure on the rail of his Maw-Maw's bed. The remote fell off the bed, hitting the hardwood floor with a loud crash. "I get it," Ben said, and hopped down. He went around the bed and gave it back to his Maw-Maw, who had opened her eyes. She smiled weakly at him and laid it back down on her bed, closing her eyes and returning to her sleep.

We had put up Beverly's favorite miniature village, an autumn scene, in her room. This now drew Ben's attention. I turned the lights on in the little village and enjoyed his gleeful expression at the sight. After 15 to 20 minutes his mom, Amy, came to say it was time to go. Believe it or not, he didn't want to leave. But the miracle—which I heard about from Amy later that night—happened on the way home.

> [He] died and was carried by the angels to Abraham's side.
>
> —LUKE 16:22 (ESV)

Ben was in his booster seat in the back of the car. "Mommy, who was that man in Maw-Maw's room?"

"What man?" There shouldn't have been any men there.

"There was a man dancing in Maw-Maw Beverly's room."

Amy remained quiet for a moment. "How was he dancing?"

With that, Ben, still in his seat, threw his arms up in the air and slowly waved them around. Then he dropped his arms and asked, "Is that man come to take Maw-Maw away?"

Now understanding who Ben had seen, Amy explained that Maw-Maw would soon be going to heaven.

Upon further questioning at home, Ben reenacted the slow, graceful dance his pure heart had witnessed—the same dance that Beverly had described to me a couple of nights before. When she shared the story with the rest of the family, we all felt comforted that God works in mysterious ways, and finds ways in His great mercy to comfort even the tiniest of hearts.

Beverly entered heaven within 48 hours of these events. God was preparing her heart to leave this world—and also preparing our hearts to let her go.

Since his Maw-Maw Beverly's homegoing, Ben still talks about "that man." Once in the car with my daughter, Ashley, he asked her if she could see "that man" and pointed out the window. It was dark, and they were driving on a country road; there was nothing anyone else could see. Ben then asked whether the man was bringing Maw-Maw back. I believe that God was still comforting Ben through His Presence.

What an amazing God we serve! After witnessing these events, I truly believe we will dance in heaven.

Not Just Another Day on the Farm

Kathleen Stauffer

I grew up on a farm where the buildings, surrounding fields, and the long lane leading to the neighbors' place were just as much a part of my heart as the house itself. My dad had spent his growing-up years there, at this same place where Mom and Dad started their married life.

One fall day, years after my father had buried his own mother, he watched her walk from one of the cornfields. She was wearing a floral dress, her thin, gray hair lightly lifted by a fall breeze. The vision was as real as day and a comfort to him although, as a man of few words, he didn't tell me that story until I was a young adult, visiting the farm during harvesttime. It gave me a sense of connection to the place just as it had done for him. To this day, the fall calls me back to the farm, a place where I always felt nurtured and cared for.

Throughout his years as a farmer he was in and out of the corncrib, the barn, the hog house, the toolshed. His steps wore a path in the fields during the various seasons as he checked on the crops or walked down the lane to get the mail. After high school, my oldest brother, Dwight, chose to help Dad with the farming operation. They were a team—working together and sharing thoughts on the weather, the markets, and what needed to be done next.

When they retired, my parents moved to a small ranch-style house in a nearby town. For over a year afterward, Dad came back to the farm each day to help in whatever way he could with the farming, arriving in a small red station wagon with his own tools in the back. My parents were practical minimalists, and never in their married years did they drive a fancy car. There were big station wagons when we were all growing up; smaller station wagons followed as empty nesting set in, almost always red.

When I visited him in assisted living, we sometimes took him for a ride to the farm. He noticed the clouds, the seasons, the crops, and spent a lot of time just looking at the countryside. The simple trip down the long lane leading to the farm brought him joy.

"Slow down. Slow down," he encouraged whoever was driving. He wanted to savor the experience of being in this place he had cared for, where he had raised his family and thought his many thoughts.

When Dad passed, just short of 100 years of age, we were saddened but also comforted that he was with Jesus, as he had desired this very thing for years. Each of us missed him in different ways, but Dwight may have been affected the most. He and Dad had worked closely together ever since Dwight

> **For God speaks again and again, though people do not recognize it. He speaks in dreams, in visions of the night, when deep sleep falls on people as they lie in their beds.**
>
> —JOB 33:14–15 (NLT)

could drive a tractor at a young age. Dwight continued to farm the land and started fixing others' farm implements in a newly installed machine shed that became known as the "shop." After Dad's death, he worked alone. There were few visitors—a fellow farmer, a rare salesman. After all, who would want to venture down such a long lane and find no one at home?

However, when working one October afternoon, Dwight heard the crunch of tires on the lane. He put his tools aside, wiped his hands on a rag, and walked to the door of the shop.

> **My Father is always at his work to this very day, and I too am working.**
>
> —JOHN 5:17 (NIV)

A large, pearly-white sedan with tinted windows came steadily up the lane. Reaching the grove, the shadows of gnarly trees slid over the car. It stopped some 25 feet from Dwight.

This close, Dwight could see that Dad was seated in the middle of the front seat, a circle of light surrounding his face. He looked directly at Dwight, smiled, and gave a slight wave of his hand before the car headed back down the drive and disappeared beneath the tree shadows.

"Dear Lord," Dwight whispered to himself, "it's Dad."

Dwight shared the story with me, weeks later, stopping occasionally to wipe a tear. The experience still has that effect on him, bringing tears to his eyes every time he tells it. He felt Dad was checking on him. Checking on him and also comforting him, sending the silent message, "I'm OK, and I see you are, too."

Vision? Dream? It was real. Just as real as Dad's own mother walking from the cornfield. These experiences offer a peace that is beyond earthly understanding and a reminder that God is constantly trying to get our attention. God understands us each intimately, and He comforts us in a way that is just right for each of us.

I'm sure Dad often felt this awesome wonder as God worked in his life—that the Creator of the universe would take notice of the life of an ordinary, soft-spoken farmer. Through the way my father lived, the way he loved his family and the land, he showed us how to interpret life from God's perspective.

Because of the example my father set and the experiences he shared, now my family can live with that understanding that God knows us intimately and likes to work in our lives. Truly, everyone can live with that knowledge. God might show up in any way He chooses—through visions, dreams, gentle urgings, or even a thunderbolt, each event uniquely planned. He controls every detail of human history, and yet He is accessible to all of us. Therefore, let us live expectantly.

An Angel in Dickies
Susan Shumway

My father passed in 1990 after a heart attack that took him from us suddenly. There was no warning, no goodbyes. At the time the only grandchildren he had were my daughter and son, ages 3 and 5. He loved them immensely, and I was blessed to witness a very precious moment between my father and my children the day before his massive heart attack.

That day had started out like any day. My father was finishing some home improvements, and the last thing on the list was having a concrete garage floor and driveway poured. I decided I would take the children to my parents' house to watch the big cement truck.

We arrived just as they were finishing, and the men left for the day. The garage floor was wet, and my father asked if we could put the children's handprints in the cement. They were so excited. I watched as my father took their hands and pressed their little palms into the cement, then wrote the date underneath the handprints. He then took the children over to the outside water faucet and lovingly washed their hands, drying each part carefully with the big handkerchief he kept in his back pocket. Watching them, my eyes filled with tears. I think God allowed me to be a quiet witness to this moment—which would be the last time I saw my father alive. He passed the next day.

After my father died, I talked to my children about him every day. I simply could not even entertain the thought that they wouldn't always remember him. Sadly, one day my son said to me, "Mom, I am not sure if I truly remember Papa, or if I just remember the stories you told us about him." I realized the beautiful moments that my father and I spent together, and that he spent with the children, were only my memories—my children did not actually remember them with me.

Many years passed, and life moved on. My brother and his wife waited a little later in their lives to have children, and when we found out she was pregnant, it was the most exciting thing that had happened in our family for many years. My children were 11 and 13 at that point. We awaited the arrival of this new little family member, and finally, one cold, winter day in December, I received word that my sister-in-law had gone into labor. Very early the next morning, my brother called me and announced he was the proud father of a beautiful baby girl. I woke the children and told them if they could get ready quickly for school, we could run over to the hospital and see her through the nursery window.

> **You have made them a little lower than the angels and crowned them with glory and honor.**
>
> —PSALM 8:5 (NIV)

They were dressed in record time that morning. Breakfast was finished quickly, and off to the hospital we went. This was my first niece, so I was very excited. My mother and sister joined us at the hospital, and we met this newest member of the family through the plate-glass window in the nursery. In between looking at the new arrival, I spent most of my time talking to my mom and sister. Finally, it came time to gather the children and get them to school. Nothing seemed out of the ordinary to me.

My daughter was rather quiet while we were driving. I barely noticed it; I was rushing to get them to their classes on time, and it wasn't a long trip. I assumed her mind was occupied with this new little cousin.

It was only several weeks later that my daughter came to me and said, "Mom, I need to talk to you."

I sat down with her. She began speaking in a very quiet voice. "I was afraid to say anything, but I saw Papa leaning over Lauren's bassinet in the hospital nursery."

I was speechless for a few seconds, and then finally gathered the presence of mind to ask her, "What do you mean?"

"Papa was in the nursery with Lauren, leaning down and looking at her," she said, still quiet. "He had on his Dickies"—the work pants that my father often wore—"and his blue handkerchief was hanging out of his back pocket. I could tell it was him, and I looked around at everyone standing with me and everyone was talking, and when I looked back, he was gone. But Mom, I know it was him."

I was at a loss for words. My daughter had always been an honest child, and there was no reason for her to tell a story like

> As the heavens are higher than the earth, so are my ways higher than your ways and my thoughts than your thoughts.
>
> —ISAIAH 55:9 (NIV)

GOD'S GIFT OF TOUCH
— Linda L. Kruschke —

THE HANDS OF the elderly are frequently wrinkled and dry, the marks of many years of living and hard work. To hold such a hand, full of wisdom and faith, can feel like touching the promises of God. While praying, one is blessed to connect by holding hands with those who have lifted a vast lifetime of prayers to the Lord. One does well to bring the young to place their hands in those of grandparents and elderly friends, just as the "people brought little children to Jesus for him to place his hands on them and pray for them" (Matthew 19:13, NIV).

---

that if it were not true. My father had now been gone eight years, and it was amazing that she remembered enough to identify him so easily. I asked her, "Why didn't you say anything before now?"

"Because I was afraid no one would believe me. I haven't said anything to anyone, but I just had to tell you."

She had no reason to lie or imagine seeing him there. There had been no one else in the nursery besides the nursing staff, certainly no one who looked like my father. I simply had to believe that God allowed my dad to see his new granddaughter. There is no other explanation needed. Not only was my father allowed to see the baby, but my daughter was given the chance to see the grandfather that I had been so afraid she wouldn't remember.

I can't explain what happened that day. But I believe in a God who can do all things, and I believe that time and space hold no boundaries for Him. Maybe my daughter's childlike faith was what led God to allow her to be the one to see my father. Thinking about it later, I wondered if perhaps it wasn't just a one-time visitation, but that God assigned my father to be his baby granddaughter's guardian angel. I don't know, but I'm sure God will explain it to me when I get to heaven. I am just fine with that.

Since that time, I have been a little more careful to listen to others and not question stories that speak of angels. God has told us so much in His Word, but there are unexplained secrets that have yet to be revealed. Knowing that my father was there, that he might even today be watching over my niece, is a great comfort to me.

The Voice
Alice H. Murray

What would God sound like if you could hear Him audibly? Would He have a booming voice? Would claps of thunder and bright flashes of light accompany His words? Hollywood would portray a communication from God in that sensational way. But my personal experience hearing God's voice involved no such drama.

It was a routine workday. I was driving from my office to meet with a woman in another county. As an adoption attorney, I often met with pregnant women in their homes to discuss adoptive placement when obtaining transportation to my office was difficult for them.

But I was nervous about this meeting. I could deal with a crying, upset, or emotional pregnant woman. Years of experience handling those situations rested under my belt. It was the location of this meeting, a trailer park in a remote area, that made me a bit anxious.

To say I felt uncomfortable about a meeting at a trailer park somewhere in the boonies would be an understatement. The trip itself was filled with uncertainties. I wasn't familiar with my destination or the route to get there. This journey took place pre-GPS days, so verbal directions from the birth mother served as my sole guide. Without a car, this woman didn't even drive. Could I really trust the directions she gave me? What if I got lost?

In addition to the meeting location being in an isolated area, it wasn't a particularly safe one. I would be dressed professionally, as I normally am for work—wearing a dress, hose, and high heels. Wouldn't I look painfully out of place? I didn't look forward to attention from her neighbors. What would I do if I were accosted by a suspicious person at this remote site? I couldn't run in high heels. And where could I run, anyway?

An appointment time in the middle of the day with the sun shining didn't lessen my nervousness. Trying to remain calm, cool, and collected, I gripped the steering wheel as I drove to this appointment. On the outside, I had it together, but mentally I was sweating like a timid sheep separated from its flock.

> **The gatekeeper opens the gate for him, and the sheep listen to his voice. He calls his own sheep by name and leads them out.**
>
> —JOHN 10:3 (NIV)

Tension mounted as I left visible civilization. Nothing but trees lined either side of the road. No billboards caught my eye to suggest a human presence. The lack of cars on the road reinforced my feeling of isolation. My shoulders tightened.

To my relief, I managed to find the trailer park without getting lost. My next hurdle was finding the correct place for my meeting. Slowly I drove down the dirt road into the residential area and cautiously looked around. Not a soul could be seen, and the location was eerily quiet and still. Woods surrounded the trailers, and the road sat some distance away.

Identifying the right trailer, I pulled up beside it and glanced about. Was I crazy to leave the locked safety of my vehicle?

Taking a deep breath, I took the plunge and stepped from my car. Hurrying to the door, I clutched the file for our meeting to my chest. I kept a death grip on my purse, which contained the keys to my only viable means of escape should one be required.

A smiling face opened the door in response to my knock. Once inside the birth mother's home, I could focus on the task at hand, temporarily forgetting my isolated location. Our meeting was productive and pleasant. Mission accomplished.

But the end of the meeting meant exiting the relative safety of the birth mother's trailer to go out into the big, wide, isolated world on the other side of her door. My nerves returned in force.

Once safely inside my car, I exhaled a long sigh of relief. Tension drained from my body as my car pulled out of the birth mother's neighborhood and onto the main road for the return trip to my office. All I had to do was to relax and enjoy the drive.

> **Be strong and courageous. Do not be afraid or terrified because of them, for the LORD your God goes with you; he will never leave you nor forsake you.**
>
> DEUTERONOMY 31:6 (NIV)

Thinking music would make my trip more enjoyable, I reached to turn on the radio. Before I could reach the knob, I heard a voice. A male voice. It didn't boom, and no thunderclaps or flashes of light accompanied it. Instead, it sounded as if a passenger in my car was speaking to me.

The voice asked, "Didn't you think I'd take care of you?"

I understood immediately who it was. The speaker was my Heavenly Father, chiding me for not trusting Him, injecting a little humor through His tone.

Although He didn't laugh, I knew God was smiling. His words hinted at what some people claim to be my favorite four words: "I told you so." My parents had taught me God goes with me and will never leave me or forsake me. Why, then, had I felt so alone in a remote location? God ribbed me for failing to act in accordance with what I had learned about Him.

The truth is I had *not* been alone. The God of the universe had been there with me all along. Bright flashes of light, claps of thunder, and a booming voice were not necessary to convince me God was talking to me—ME! In a moment when I felt most alone and vulnerable, God reached out to remind me that no matter which professional credentials I had or how much I'd achieved, like a little girl, I still needed Him. And He was there for me, no matter where I went. The warm feeling in my heart and the peace in my mind flowed from recognizing His presence.

In the days, months, and years that followed, I became more attuned to God's presence. I felt empowered to speak to Him—sometimes out loud!—whenever I was going through a stressful, daunting, or unknown situation. I've been able to move with more confidence knowing that He is always with me.

Looking back on this adventure, I laugh at how I acted like a scared sheep. But experiencing that fear was worth it because it led to a divine encounter. God spoke to me and assured me of His constant presence—not just in that moment, but in every moment. And this sheep knew His voice.

The Final Gift
Jeannie Hughes

I fumbled for my phone as my mother's ring tone awakened me in the middle of the night. Never good news. I answered to her panicked voice: "Jeannie, come quick. Something's wrong with your father."

"Did you call 911?" I asked.

"We're at the emergency room now. Hurry!"

I was already grabbing a pair of jeans as she talked. "I'll be right there."

The phone had woken up my teenage daughter, Lindsay. "What's wrong?" she asked.

"Your grandfather is in the ER, and I have to go there," I told her.

"I'll go too," she said, already leaving the room to get dressed.

We drove faster toward the hospital than we probably should have. Dad had been a lifelong diabetic and I pictured it being another episode of his sugar levels being out of control.

When Lindsay and I arrived at the emergency room, Dad lay still under a crisp white sheet while my mother stood at the foot of the bed. She looked at me. I recognized fear on her face.

Mom said, "I thought it must be his sugar and gave him a hamburger to eat. He tried, but he couldn't."

A doctor rushed into the room, so fast that I could feel the breeze wash across my face as he hurried past me.

"What's going on?" I asked.

"We're taking him to intensive care. He's had a stroke." The doctor spoke as quickly as he walked.

"You mean he's going to die?" my mother asked.

Ignoring her question, attendants zipped Dad away into a room. We followed and were told to wait outside the closed door. No one came to talk to us and let us know what was going on.

> **The one who was dying blessed me; I made the widow's heart sing.**
>
> —JOB 29:13 (NIV)

Finally, the door opened. Doctors and nurses filed out. *All those people for one man? Not good,* I thought. One nurse remained behind, adjusting his blood pressure cuff.

Mom went in the room first and sat in one of the visitor chairs. The rest of us followed. Dad had been hooked up to so many machines, tubes seemed to run from every inch of his body.

"What's screwed into his head?" I asked.

The nurse turned and hesitated. I could tell she wanted to get one of the doctors. "Well, he had fluid in his brain, and this will help drain it off," she said. "A doctor will be in shortly to talk with you." Then, once again, it was the three of us staring at Dad.

"I think the machines are the only thing keeping him alive," my daughter said. I couldn't help but think the same thing.

It took nearly an hour of waiting, but a doctor finally entered the room. He wasn't in a hurry like the other one. He sat and talked to Mom, explaining how the stroke had been in the brain stem and how very sorry he was.

"I don't think there is anything else we can do for him. You need to tell me what you want me to do. Should we keep him on the machines?" the doctor asked.

Mom turned to me. "Jeannie, what should I do?"

"Doctor, my father already made that decision. He has a living will. He didn't want any life-saving measures taken. You've already done more than he wanted," I said.

"I understand. Someone will be right in to remove all of this," he said.

"How long does it usually take?" I asked.

"Sometimes a few minutes. Sometimes several hours for the organs to shut down," he told us.

After the doctor left, my mother took all of her fear and anger out on me. "You killed him! He'd still keep on living if you hadn't told them to take him off life support! Miracles happen! Who are you to say a miracle wasn't going to bring him back?" Mom shouted at me. I understood. She was just scared.

We left the room so the staff could move my father to a comfort bed. When they had gotten him settled in, the three of us just sat in burgundy chairs and watched Dad's labored breathing. I looked at the clock hanging on the wall. It reminded me of the one I used to watch in grade school, willing the hands to turn faster. Nothing could help Dad now. I would not want family watching me linger.

An hour had gone by. The second hand on the clock turned slowly. We talked in hushed tones, always aware of the slightest change in Dad's breathing.

After a tiring six hours, I turned to my mother. "Mom, he has always listened to you. I think it's time you tried whispering in his ear that it's OK for him to go."

She shook her head. "I can't do that. Obviously, it's not his time yet."

"I think Dad's only waiting for permission from you."

Mom waited a few moments. I was beginning to think she wasn't going to do it. Then, as if accepting her fears, she approached my father. She walked slowly, like she was gathering in her mind what she was going to say.

> I will show wonders in the heavens above and signs on the earth below, blood and fire and billows of smoke.
>
> —ACTS 2:19 (NIV)

My daughter and I heard her speak, in a gentle whisper, as she stroked the top of his head. She told him of everyone he would see in heaven. How his mom was waiting for him and what a glorious homecoming it would be. "It's OK. I'll be fine. It's time," she said to him.

She walked back to her chair. "Was that all right?"

"You did great," my daughter said.

We all held hands, expecting something, but not knowing what. At that moment, my breath caught in my throat.

A thin wisp of what looked like a circling white cloud floated up from my dad's chest toward the ceiling. We sat in awe. It couldn't have lasted more than several heartbeats, but it seemed to go on for minutes.

"Do either of you see that?" I asked softly.

"You mean the mist?" my daughter answered in a hushed tone.

I took a quick glance at my mother. Her eyes were huge and her mouth open. When I saw her nod her head in agreement, I knew she had witnessed the amazing miracle also.

After it was over, the three of us sat in silence, each lost in her own thoughts about what had just happened. We were in no hurry to call for a nurse. We knew Dad was gone. He had left us with the greatest gift of all—one final goodbye, and the knowledge that angels were guiding his spirit to heaven.

If instead of a gem, or even a flower, we should cast the gift of a loving thought into the heart of a friend, that would be giving as the angels give.

—George MacDonald

CHAPTER 7

God's Human Angels

Blood Kin 210
  Roberta Messner

Angels on the Road to Beit El. 214
  Miriam Green

An Angel in My Garden 219
  Linda VanderWier

Rescued on the Road. 225
  Wendy Klopfenstein

Life Is an Adventure 231
  Patricia Cameron

The 8-Year Project 235
  Renee Mitchell

A Second Chance 240
  Felicia Harris-Russell

Blood Kin
Roberta Messner

I was seeing my last patient when the call came. "About your surgery," a nurse was saying. "There's no B negative blood to be had. The Red Cross doesn't have any, or the plasma center... There's just *none*."

The word "none" hung in the silence of the now-empty VA exam room, taunting me. I felt my palms grow clammy. If there was *none*, there could be no surgery to remove the large painful tumor behind my eye. I'd hemorrhaged during a similar operation three years before. They weren't taking any chances this time.

I'd had it all planned out. Signed up to give my own blood. Autologous, they called it. That was me, all right. I got things done on my own. Until they pronounced my hemoglobin levels "too puny."

"Any way *you* could find donors?" the nurse asked. "It's your only hope with a blood type as rare as yours."

"We need twelve people with B negative blood?" I wailed into the phone. "How? My surgery's next week!"

These were the days before social media. That evening I dialed up everyone I could think of who might know someone with my precious blood type. With one phone call, I'd gone from self-sufficient to bumming blood.

My efforts turned up nothing. But the next afternoon at the hospital, I got another call, this time from the American Red Cross. They had a dozen donors for me.

"How?" I asked, stunned.

"One of your veterans heard you say you needed blood and just had to do something," the lady told me. Turned out he'd canvassed all of the patient waiting rooms, then rallied the troops at the Veterans of Foreign Wars, the Disabled American Veterans, and the American Legion. "They all showed up here this morning," she said. "Every last one of them B negative, with hemoglobin levels strong enough to donate."

America's veterans are some of the most compassionate and loving folks around. Of like mind and spirit. But I'd never heard of anything like this. And for *me*. The very thought of it!

> **How good and pleasant it is when God's people live together in unity!**
>
> —PSALM 133:1 (NIV)

They scheduled my personal blood drive on the grounds of our VA hospital, so I went out to meet them and say thank you. Tacked on a tree was a poster complete with a photo of me and one of our patients. I imagined a knot of veterans gathering to read: "Blood drive for Nurse Roberta today. Got B negative? She's our type!"

When I went inside and found the group, their voices were filled with joy as they waited to be called into service: "You'll have courage when you get *my* blood," a guy who'd traveled 2 hours from deep in Kentucky said. "You'll never give up," echoed another. "Or stop laughing," a guy in a black leather biker jacket promised. "When you have mine, you'll be riding a Harley and smoking unfiltered Camels."

I surveyed the amazing crowd. "How did you ever pull this off?" I asked the patient who had organized the whole thing.

"Marched right down to the Red Cross and asked to see the Top Dog. Real swell lady. She took it from there." (It was only years later that I would learn the identity of the lady they called "Top Dog"—Pauline Kaplan, who'd served as the administrator of the American Red Cross for 40 years.)

I entered the mobile unit where the blood was being drawn, and the first thing I saw was a nurse with a tourniquet standing over an outstretched burly arm. I was too overwhelmed to look at the face the arm belonged to. "Thank you!" I finally managed.

A deep voice turned the pages of time. "Remember me, Roberta? It's Joe. You shaved me after my big cancer surgery." I'd been the new nurse who snagged that razor in the folds of his face. Sick as he was, Joe had worried about *me*. Taught me how torn pieces of toilet tissue could stop the bleeding and no one would be the wiser. His belly had started to pain him, but when I handed him a mirror, he broke out in a grin at the speckles of white. "This face has seen a lot of miles," he told me. "Not all of 'em paved." So raw and real. Humble.

I studied his face, this time reading between those lines. Determination lived there. Heart and soul. Tested-in-the-foxholes faith. Qualities he'd share with me when his blood ran through my veins.

The evening after my surgery, a team of doctors filed into my room. The attending beamed. "Your operation couldn't have gone better, Roberta!" he said. "We got most of the tumor and you hardly bled at all. You didn't need a single transfusion."

My doctors left smiling, but my face refused to budge. Sure, I was glad about the tumor. But what about all those veterans who'd been so excited to give me their blood?

Seeing my expression, the lady from housekeeping eyed me warily. She came closer, leaning on her mop. "My surgery went great!" I ventured, the sick feeling in my stomach taking over.

"I heard that," she said. "Now tell me what you're really thinking."

It all poured out. The hopes and dreams of all my veteran patients for me. My dreams, too. "How will I ever tell them I didn't need their gifts?" I said. The blood bond they'd talked about wouldn't come to pass now. "I'll never have their courage, their strength, their humor, their sense of adventure."

> **Finally, all of you, be like-minded, be sympathetic, love one another, be compassionate and humble.**
>
> —1 PETER 3:8 (NIV)

She came closer to my bed, leaned on the siderail, her eyes searching mine. "My boy served in Vietnam," she said. "I've been around a lot of veterans, honey. They're just-in-case folks. When they leave home, they don't know how they're coming back or if they're coming back at all. It's a gift, just in case." She stroked my arm, her words as soft as her touch. "You already have their qualities, just by knowing them."

All these years later, I still feel the truth of that, no matter what life tries to send my way. In the 38 years I was honored to be a VA nurse, my angels on standby made me stronger, more courageous, hopeful—everything they promised.

And always up for adventure. Though I've passed on the Harley and those unfiltered Camels!

Angels on the Road to Beit El

Miriam Green

I never expected to find angels in Judea and Samaria, but maybe I should have.

We were on our way to Beit El, the city named after the site where Jacob slept and dreamed of angels going up and down a heavenly ladder (Genesis 28:19). We'd been invited by my niece Eliana to attend the *pidyon haben* ceremony of our first grandnephew.

The place of a firstborn son holds great importance in Judaism. In traditional societies, eldest sons have special power and respect. By virtue of their birth, they're in charge of the family's money and property. Birth order determines the allocation of a double portion of the family's inheritance (as prescribed in Deuteronomy 21:17), and the nation of Israel as a whole is prophetically called God's firstborn.

The *pidyon haben*, a ceremony to redeem the firstborn son, is a rare practice. It isn't performed if the firstborn is a girl, if the child is born via caesarian section, if this child's birth was preceded by a miscarriage, or if either grandfather carries the status of a *kohen* or a Levite. Any of these specific circumstances exempt the family from the obligation to perform the *pidyon haben* ritual.

The exact meaning behind the *mitzvah* (religious duty) of *pidyon haben,* and what the son is being redeemed from, can vary depending on whom you ask. Some think it's about redeeming a son from the stigma of the last of the Ten Plagues in ancient Egypt. Others see it as a way to free the son from his duty to serve as a priest. It's fascinating how people can have different interpretations of the same tradition. To fulfill this mitzvah, a payment of five silver coins is ceremonially made to a patrilineal descendant of the priestly family of Aaron.

Eliana had lucked out. All the necessary requirements had lined up, and we were as excited as she was to be celebrating this special occasion.

That was how we found ourselves traveling from our home in Beer Sheva one night with our children and our youngest niece, driving along the curved, dusty roads from Jerusalem to Beit El.

> **He had a dream; a stairway was set on the ground and its top reached the sky, and angels of God were going up and down on it.**
>
> —GENESIS 28:12 (JPS)

Night driving in any unfamiliar area can be difficult. We weren't exactly sure of the way and didn't want to end up in the wrong place. Add to that the tensions that exist between Israelis and Palestinians in Judea and Samaria—or what is commonly called the West Bank—and driving into the wrong village could get you stoned . . . or worse. There had been so many incidents of violence against Israelis driving in that region that I gritted my teeth the whole time, my hand cramping as I held on to the door handle. Stones thrown at cars can be lethal.

We took a wrong turn.

In the pitch black, Israeli soldiers stopped us at the checkpoint to a Palestinian village. With guns in hand, they gestured to my husband, Jeff, to roll down the window. They knew immediately that we were Israeli from our car's license plates.

"Where do you think you're going?" they snapped at us, bulky in helmets, flak jackets, and machine guns, their luminous faces green with camouflage.

Realizing we were lost, the soldiers told us to turn around and gave us directions to get to where we were going. Jeff maneuvered the car on the narrow two-way road, blocking traffic in both directions as the car slowly rotated around. Our headlights lit up swaths of the road, the surrounding hills, the soldiers, and the impatient Palestinian villagers in the other cars.

It felt like we were in the midst of an awful dream. As we got our bearings, I looked into the eyes of the soldiers and imagined the kindness behind their steely gazes. I glimpsed masks on the faces of some villagers. *Why is there so much hate and fear?* I asked myself. The dark land was bejeweled with lights, their cities identical to ours.

Angels, I thought, knowing that the soldiers had prevented us from entering a no-go zone and a possible tragedy. The Arabs don't take too kindly to lost Israelis.

That's when—for some strange reason I can no longer recall—my son Rafi and niece Avigyle decided to argue about what angels are. Are they separate beings with corporeal form? Or embodiments of God's emotions? Rafi, in sixth grade, and Avigyle, in fifth, were good friends and very competitive. They both studied in public religious schools, and in addition to the mainstay subjects of English, math, and geography, they got a good dose of Torah learning.

The Hebrew term for angel, *malach*, carries a profound meaning: messenger. It speaks of beings who serve as conduits of divine purpose, bearing messages of hope, guidance, and grace from God to our world. Each angel embodies a unique facet of God's love and justice, with Michael radiating kindness, Gabriel enacting judgments, and Rafael extending healing hands to the wounded souls.

Imagine the intensity of angels' lives—their very essence shaped by the tasks they're assigned, their purpose etched into their being. Some are formed for singular missions, their existence like shooting stars illuminating the night sky.

In Jewish tradition there's another kind of angel, born not of celestial decree but of human action. Through our deeds—both virtuous and flawed—we sculpt angels of advocacy or accusation. With each *mitzvah* fulfilled, an angelic advocate emerges, standing by our side, while each transgression calls forth an angelic accuser, a haunting reminder of our failings.

> **An angel of the Lord appeared to [Moses] in a blazing fire out of a bush. He gazed, and there was a bush all aflame, yet the bush was not consumed.**
>
> —EXODUS 3:2 (JPS)

But there's more to angels than celestial messengers. In Jewish teachings, they embody the very laws of nature, the unseen hands guiding the universe according to God's divine plan. They are reminders that even in the mundane, God's presence is palpable.

In our prayers, we acknowledge these celestial beings, their voices lifted in harmonious praise before the Divine throne. Picture them, their ethereal melodies echoing through the cosmos, their song a symphony of adoration and reverence.

And consider the urgency, the passion, behind their existence. In the stories from the Torah, we see glimpses of their dedication—the angel pleading with Jacob, yearning to fulfill its duty before the break of dawn, or the shifting melodies guiding Moses through his sacred communion with God.

In every whisper of prayer, every moment of study, every act of kindness, we invite these angels into our lives, weaving their presence into the fabric of our existence. They are more than messengers; they are companions on our journey, witnesses to our joys and sorrows, our triumphs and tribulations. When we embrace their presence, we find a glimpse of the divine, a reminder that we are never truly alone on this winding path of life.

As we drove away, I felt the angels guiding us, the car skating on a thread of shining road.

An Angel in My Garden

Linda VanderWier

Not all angels live in heaven. Some reside, unbeknownst to us, in our own neighborhoods. We didn't know we had one living across the street from us until July of 1983.

The summer started uneventfully. I had finished a year of teaching, and my brothers had each finished another year of college and high school. Since we were all living at home with our parents, we understood we needed to pitch in and help with chores. Working in our fair-sized garden kept all of us busy. By June, our vegetable seeds had sprouted promisingly. The fence had successfully kept hungry critters from munching on the young plants. To all appearances, we would soon enjoy a bountiful harvest of vegetables.

But my brothers and I were busy with more than just gardening that summer. We'd been secretly planning a party for our parents' twenty-fifth wedding anniversary in August, meeting quietly at night to keep our intentions a surprise. Our folks deserved the most royal of celebrations, and we planned to give them the best. Our friends and family loved them and were eager to help us. By early July, we had most details arranged and were getting excited. Everything was running on schedule. The countdown was on.

Then, early one Sunday morning, as I was getting ready to leave for church, the telephone rang. Our phone didn't usually ring on Sunday mornings, so, curious, I hurried to answer it.

I didn't recognize the voice on the other end of the line. The caller identified himself as a doctor, and he asked for a Mr. "Somebody"—I didn't recognize the name. I told him he had the wrong number, he apologized, and we ended the call.

Within seconds, I heard my mother shouting frantically from the bottom of the stairs.

> **Be not forgetful to entertain strangers: for thereby some have entertained angels unawares.**
>
> —HEBREWS 13:2 (KJV)

"Who was that on the phone?"

"Just a wrong number," I called back, coming to the stairs so we didn't have to yell.

The answer didn't satisfy her. "What did he want?"

"A doctor. I didn't recognize the name. He asked for someone who doesn't live here."

"Well, what did you do?"

I was puzzled. Why would she ask that? "Obviously he had a wrong number. I told him so and hung up."

I could tell from her expression that was not the answer she had hoped for, which left me even more baffled.

If I'd had a clue what had taken place in my folks' bedroom that morning, I would have understood—that "wrong number" was a doctor, and he was calling with important news. Later, my brothers and I would find out that my father had been dealing with concerning physical issues for some time, but hadn't told us. All we knew that morning was what my mother told me: Dad was very sick, and he needed to go to a hospital.

The next hour became a blur. My brothers carefully assisted my father to the car, and my mother drove off to the hospital with him. My brothers and I stood staring after them, shocked. Our father had seemed so strong, so healthy. How could he be sick?

As she'd driven off, Mom had told us to go to church like normal. The day felt far from normal, but, in obedience and complete confusion, we headed for Sunday school. After class, we called the hospital from the church phone. Mom's voice conveyed her anxiety. Even without details, we knew the news would not be good. We tried to reassure her and told her we'd get to the hospital as soon as church ended.

A couple of days later, after running numerous tests, doctors gave us the news we'd most feared—Dad had cancer. The shock felt cold. Surreal. Surely my father couldn't have such a horrible disease. But no there was no question: he had colon cancer, and the tumor had ruptured through the colon wall, sparking the sudden downturn on Sunday morning. Surgery was scheduled and took place several days later.

> **As we have therefore opportunity, let us do good unto all men, especially unto them who are of the household of faith.**
>
> —GALATIANS 6:10 (KJV)

Mom rarely left Dad's side in that sterile hospital room throughout the testing, surgery, or his recovery. My siblings and I tried to care for her as she maintained vigil with Dad. The hospital kept Dad fed; we kept Mom fed. Between our working hours, we ran errands and kept family, friends, and neighbors as informed as possible. Several people kindly offered to help, but at the time we felt too overwhelmed to understand our own needs.

We eventually remembered our garden. We knew we'd never be able to keep up with it. By that time, produce was heavy on the plants: green beans, cucumbers, beets, peas, scads of tomatoes, zucchini, and much more. Our meals during that time were more fast food than full meals. We were not cooking anything at home. So, after talking through the situation, Mom decided to offer the produce to the folks in our small neighborhood. She asked the Babbs—the neighbors who lived directly across the street—to let the neighbors know our garden was open to any who could use the vegetables. And then, in the rush of caring for Mom and Dad, we didn't give the garden another thought.

One week later, Dad came home from the hospital. His surgery had gone well. The cancer had been encapsulated, and the doctors believed they had gotten it all. Thirteen months of chemotherapy was scheduled. But, though we'd received hope from the doctors' reports, our heads continued to reel. Our lives had changed.

Shortly after bringing Dad home, Mom strolled out to the garden. What she saw must have shocked her. The garden was stripped bare. There was not a single ripe tomato, bean, cucumber, or any other vegetables to be seen. The neighbors had obviously been delighted to have the fresh garden goods offered to them. Mom had fully intended for them to help themselves to all they could use—it was better than leaving the produce to rot on the vine—but I believe she'd have been happy to see just one tomato or cucumber peeking out from behind a leaf.

She didn't mind. The produce had not gone to waste during our time away, and the garden would not soon need tending. We could all concentrate on Dad.

A few weeks later, we heard a quiet knock on our front door. It was our neighbor, Mrs. Babb. She was carrying a large box and asked if she could bring it into the house.

We certainly didn't expect what it held. In our absence, Mrs. Babb had come to our garden and picked all the ripened produce. But her family hadn't eaten it. Instead, she had washed and blanched the produce, placing them in storage bags and then freezing them until she felt we were settled into our new routine. And now here she was on our front porch with a box of our own produce to fill our freezer!

Never had I heard of such an unselfish act of love and service. I don't believe the idea would ever have crossed my own mind to do such a kindness.

> **Bear ye one another's burdens, and so fulfill the law of Christ.**
>
> —GALATIANS 6:2 (KJV)

As we loaded the food into our big freezer, we couldn't get over what Mrs. Babb had done for us. I'm sure we convinced her to keep some bags for her family, but we knew nothing could repay her for the time and energy she'd put into preserving that food for us.

The summer concluded with a wonderful, though lower-key version, of the anniversary celebration my brothers and I had planned. The outpouring of love from friends and neighbors rallied our spirits. God gave Dad and Mom thirty-seven more anniversaries, allowing them to celebrate a total of 62 years together. Dad lived to meet and enjoy all my grandchildren. But through the years, none of us has ever forgotten the blessing of the angel in our garden that summer long ago.

I have seen true love in action.

GOD'S GIFT OF TASTE
— Kimberly Shumate —

IN MATTHEW 5:13 (NIV), Jesus says, "You are the salt of the earth." What a precious commodity to compare us to, especially given the time it was written. Salt was an important preservative and disinfectant, and it was scarce enough to be used as currency. Jesus places us in that category. When we follow Him, when we reflect Him to those around us, we preserve His ministry, add personality to the gospel message, and embody the heavy price He paid to make it possible. As Christ's "salt," we season the world—just as Jesus did.

Angels don't always have wings, but they surround us. They perform the kindnesses God places on their hearts. They show up with goodness in their hands on the front porch. With unexpected acts in unexpected ways at unexpected times, they do the work of God to bring comfort to the hearts of those who need it most.

Mrs. Babb's kind gesture encouraged me to be creative in considering where I can perform my own acts of kindness. I doubt I'll ever do anything as spectacular as she did, but I'm certainly looking for my opportunity to serve as God's messenger of love to someone in need.

Rescued on the Road
Wendy Klopfenstein

I glanced at the digital clock on the dash of my Pontiac Grand Am as I nervously shifted in my seat. There were only 10 minutes left to get back to work in time from lunch. Nothing in me wanted a reprimand for tardiness. But if all went according to plan, I'd have just enough time.

The office building where I worked was in the greater Oklahoma City area. I followed the familiar four-lane road—two lanes in each direction—congested with the noon traffic, as I weaved my way back to the office. In front of me in the left-hand lane, a car stopped with its left turn signal blinking, waiting to cross the two lanes of oncoming traffic and pull into a parking lot across the street. My pulse raced as a line of cars stacked into a row behind me, all of them as impatient as I was to get to their destination. As tensions rose, traffic pulled around me to fly past my car in the right-hand lane, leaving me no way to move over.

I let out a huff of frustration as I waited for the vehicle ahead of me to get a break and turn. This hadn't been part of my plan. I knew better than to cut my return from the lunch hour so close.

Finally, the vehicle ahead of me moved out of the way as it turned across traffic. In relief, I shifted my foot from the brake to the accelerator, only to find my car didn't budge. I scanned the dash. No warning lights blinked. No smoke barreled from the hood. Then I realized that there were also no lights, not even the clock. My car had died. I was stranded in the middle of a four-lane road in the rush of lunch-hour traffic.

Letting out a deep breath, I turned the key in the ignition. The blare of horns from behind me blended with the whooshing of cars passing in close proximity from the oncoming lanes. The impatience all around me was palpable. My fingers trembled as they gripped the key still sitting in the ignition.

"Come on. Come on." I pleaded with the engine to turn over, but to no avail. At 21, I had little to no knowledge of what to do with a stalled car that wouldn't start again. I couldn't see a way out of this.

"Lord, I need your help." I breathed the prayer, trying to calm my panic.

Then I remembered my cell phone. I dug through my purse to find my phone, my hand shaking as cars swooshed by me on all sides.

Before I had time to punch in a number, I spotted movement in the rearview mirror. A man had parked behind me and exited his car. He approached my driver's side window, careful of the oncoming traffic. Unable to roll down my windows with the car dead, I opened my door a crack to talk to him. I figured anyone walking the fine line between my car and the oncoming traffic must be wanting to help.

"What's wrong?" He probably wondered if I'd run out of gas.

"I don't know. It just died." I had to raise my voice to be heard above the traffic.

"First things first. Let's get you out of the road." His head turned left and right, scanning the sides of the street. He looked back at me, then pointed to the asphalt parking lot on the opposite side of the road. "It'll be easier to push it off this way.

When a break in the oncoming traffic opens up, I'll push and you steer."

I nodded my head and watched as he jogged back to position himself behind the car. Once he was in place, I waited for a break in the traffic. Palms sweating as I clung to the steering wheel, my eyes darted back and forth from the traffic to the man behind me. When the oncoming traffic slowed, I readied myself to steer, but the car never moved.

My Good Samaritan jogged back up beside the driver's door, sweat beading on his forehead. "Do you have it in neutral?"

Neutral? I didn't even know what neutral was for, much less think about using it. My face heated with embarrassment at having made things harder for the kind man trying to help me.

"Sorry." I shook my head and quickly moved the shifter until the red mark lined up with the capital N. The next opening in traffic, my Good Samaritan pushed, the car budged, and we were off. In a matter of minutes, he had rolled my car out of the road and into a side parking lot.

> **Do not forget to show hospitality to strangers, for by so doing some people have shown hospitality to angels without knowing it.**
>
> —HEBREWS 13:2 (NIV)

With the vehicle safely out of the way, he jogged back across the road to get his own car. As I watched from the driver's seat of my car, I put in a call to my mother to let her know what was going on. We planned for me to wait until she arrived to have AAA tow it for us. Then I called my manager at work.

Much to my relief, she was sympathetic. A car dead in the road was reason enough to be late.

As my shoulders began to relax, a tap sounded on the window.

"Do you need a ride anywhere?" The man, now parked beside me, had come over to check on me again.

I weighed my options before agreeing to get in his car. Surely the man who had patiently helped me this far would be safe to take a ride from, but I paused anyway. When I didn't get any clench in the gut, I smiled.

"Please. I work just up the street."

"No problem."

I locked my car and climbed into the passenger side of my Good Samaritan's vehicle, then gave him directions to the office building where I worked. As he drove, I called my mother again to let her know the change of plans. We decided to get the car after work. I breathed a sigh of relief. I'd only be a little late today.

Silence filled the car as I pointed to the next turn.

"You know, I wasn't going to stop." The man threw me a glance, then focused back on the road. "But when I drove past and saw the panic on your face, I had to turn around and help."

I chuckled inside. How many people confessed to struggling with lending a hand? I knew why he turned around. His decision to help was an answer to prayer.

> **Cast your cares on the LORD and he will sustain you; he will never let the righteous be shaken.**
>
> —PSALM 55:22 (NIV)

"I'm so glad you did. Thank you." Silently, I thanked the Lord for sending this Good Samaritan, even if he had been unwilling at first.

He pulled into the parking lot of the office where I worked. I thanked him profusely as I climbed out of the car. The glass windows of the one-story office building reflected my weary, although relieved, smile back at me. When he pulled away, part of me wondered if I'd seen an angel unaware.

I stepped into the office lined with cubicles. My manager was thrilled to have me back at my desk so quickly. So was the coworker who had relieved me at the switchboard for lunch. That afternoon, my parents surprised me by getting the car towed to the shop while I was still at work. In a matter of days, my car was running again. All seemed right in my world.

> **Because you are my help, I sing in the shadow of your wings.**
>
> —PSALM 63:7 (NIV)

About a week later, I stopped in to shop at a large warehouse club in the area. Garbled words sounded over the loudspeaker as I rounded an aisle with my cart. I looked up just in time to avoid running into my Good Samaritan.

His face lit with recognition. "How's your car?"

"It's fixed now. The mechanics said the alternator probably went out when I stopped for the car in front of me. That's what caused my car to die on the road."

"I figured it must be the alternator or the battery. I'm glad you got it running again."

"I can't thank you enough for all your help that day."

"It was no problem. This is my wife." He turned to introduce me to the lovely woman beside him. "Honey, this is the girl I told you about."

After a little more small talk, we parted ways. I don't remember getting my Good Samaritan's name. But I will never forget being 21, running late for work, and having my car break down. Nor will I ever forget how a stranger, despite the danger and inconvenience, refused to ignore the urge to stop for the panicked young woman stuck in the middle of the road.

Life Is an Adventure
Patricia Cameron

It wasn't the adventure I had imagined.

The six of us—me, my two elderly parents, and my three teenage children—drove northwest on a foggy, rainy morning after a 2-day visit to Branson, Missouri. The stop had marked the halfway point of our trip from our home in Louisiana to Concordia, Kansas, to take my parents to visit the first place they lived after they married. Taking our time to see the sights on the way, we had stopped in Joplin, Missouri, that morning and then headed toward Wichita, Kansas, where we planned to spend the night before making the remaining 2-hour trek north to Concordia the next day. We anticipated a relaxing evening eating a steak dinner in Wichita, even calling to make dinner reservations on the way.

We stopped for gas and a rest break about an hour from Wichita. The trip spiraled downhill from there. As I turned off the car, an alarm warned the car remote was missing. I didn't worry immediately, as I thought it had just slipped off the console. That had happened to me a couple of times in the past, so I knew all I had to do was find it and move it closer to the ignition.

That theory fell short when a search of the floor revealed only loose change and trash scattered from our 4 days on the road.

I remembered using the fob to unlock the car from a distance at our last stop, but my memory ended there. We never did figure out what happened to it, and without that remote, the car simply wouldn't start—a safety feature that had suddenly become a major problem.

After an hour-long wait at the gas station, my OnStar representative failed to locate an Uber or Lyft driver to pick us up and take us to Wichita. My mind began to search for a solution. What was I going to do with my two elderly parents and three teenagers stuck in the middle of nowhere?

We found a company to tow the car. The driver suggested a closer drop-off location and hotel than the ones we'd originally been heading for. He kindly offered us a ride with him; however, Dad couldn't make it up into the tow truck, and there were six of us, a mobility scooter, and a week's worth of luggage that needed to be transported. Picture the family of *Home Alone* at the airport—except bags piled outside a small gas station.

> **Let each of you look not only to his own interests, but also to the interests of others.**
>
> —PHILIPPIANS 2:4 (ESV)

Desperate to get my parents settled into a hotel for the night, I took the suggestion of the nice ladies working at the gas station and called the local county sheriff's office. The sergeant I spoke to turned me down at first. But, as we learned later, one of their two deputies was sitting at a computer near the sergeant and heard the phone call. She knew he wanted to help, but he didn't think they had a vehicle equipped to handle the mobility scooter. She remembered that the department had an inmate transport van that was rarely used. She had recently driven it, or she never would have thought about the van. When she shared her idea, the sergeant agreed to let her pick us up and take us 40 miles to the nearest town.

The deputy made conversation the entire way, putting us at ease as well as teasing my boys about the ankle cuffs in the back seat. We even have pictures to prove it. As former deputy sheriffs, my mom and I had much in common to talk about with her.

Our newfound friend told us that she didn't mind going out of her way to help because she knew how it felt to be stranded. She took a lot of her personal time to drive an hour to pick us up and then 45 minutes in a different direction to get us to a hotel. Her kindness touched my family, and to this day I believe God dispatched her to help us— our angel in uniform.

> And Jesus said to him, "You go, and do likewise."
>
> —LUKE 10:37 (ESV)

Four hours after our initial stop, we walked into the hotel lobby, grateful for a bed and roof over our heads.

The next day, after waiting several hours for a new car key to be made, I picked up my parents and sons at the hotel at 2 o'clock. I asked my mom whether she wanted to continue with the rest of the trip or begin the drive back toward home. The trip had been intended as a gift for her and Dad, so I wanted to take their feelings into account.

She was ready to release me from responsibility, knowing we were now many hours behind schedule. "It's late. We can head home."

I thought for a moment. Even though she'd been willing to stop, I knew that my mom, who never asks for anything, really wanted to visit the first town she and dad lived in after they married. "No, we've come this far. We're going."

We drove the final two hours to Concordia. But after all the adventures that we'd been through to get there, it was only after we arrived that we realized that neither Mom nor Dad remembered how to get to the house where they'd lived! We drove downtown looking for a house with the distinctive basement entrance—the entrance to the little apartment they'd been renting—that they might recognize.

We never did find that house. But my 90-year-old dad directed us right to the oil field where he had worked. He pointed out the end of the field where their drilling rig had been. He smiled and laughed because he was still able to find it after 62 years. I smiled and laughed because God gave me a memory I'd never forget.

And it was all because of a blessing I received from a deputy who turned out to be an angel in disguise. Because she'd had the experience of being stranded, she went out of her way to help us. And because of the way she helped us, I won't think twice about being the hands—or wheels—for someone else in need.

The 8-Year Project
Renee Mitchell

My husband, Larry, and I purchased my grandmother's home for $1 in 1982. We knew the house would need a lot of work when we bought it, but as soon as we tore out the first wall, we understood that the restoration was going to take even more hard work, patience, and faith than we had imagined. We were just starting out, and didn't have much money, so we leaned on the Lord for everything. And we found out how God would use this huge project to enrich our lives as well as those He brought our way.

On one particular Saturday, we were outside the house tearing off siding. We were early risers, so it was around 7 a.m. Our home was on a dirt road, and when someone was coming up the road you could spot them a mile away. This time the cloud of dust turned out to be three trucks pulling in. Men, women, and children jumped out and began unloading tools.

Larry and I shared a quick glance at each other and then made our way over to the new arrivals. Among the crew were our cousins James and Tracy, along with Kenneth and Calvin, my cousins by marriage. They had brought ice chests and food for the day.

Tracy knew me so well. She understood without asking that I would feel overwhelmed by all the work that lay ahead of us. Looking straight at me, she said, "We have enough food for an army. Don't worry about a thing." It was one of our first experiences with people just showing up, and it felt humbling to realize they had given up time with their families to help us.

Before we knew it, a radio was blaring with beautiful worship music and the hammers were swinging. Our hearts were so full. We couldn't help but praise the Father for what He had done. As we took our lunch break, I looked around. It was amazing to see how many people were sitting, talking, and laughing, excited about what we had just accomplished. Larry bowed his head to pray over the food and the wonderful people who had come. The tears flowed from our eyes as we thanked God for His goodness. We worked several more hours that day—but that was just the beginning. Those same people came over and over until the outside of our home was complete.

We felt God's love again when it came time for the electrical to be put in. We had saved our money, knowing it would be an expensive project, and prayed from the beginning that it wouldn't go over the budget we had allowed. When we were ready, we hired Ron, a member of our church and someone we had been friends with for most of our lives. He came and worked diligently for four days. We fed him and made sure that he had everything he needed. In between the work, we spent hours each day talking about the things of God and how the Lord was at work in many areas of our lives. Each night as he left, we would pray together over him and his family.

On the last day, when all was done, Ron's wife came by. She shared with me how he had talked with her each night about how he felt God had brought him to our home. Unable to hold back tears, I told her that we too had benefited spiritually through the fellowship each day. It was obvious the Lord had planned for this time together.

As we said our goodbyes, Larry handed Ron payment for the service he had done. The two of them embraced, and Larry felt something in his hand. Ron had torn up the check and handed it back to him.

We just stood there. It was hundreds of dollars, one of the most expensive projects we needed to complete on our home. Larry protested, "We can't let you do all of this work and not pay you for your labor!"

"God blessed me through this whole experience," Ron replied. "I want to share the blessing with you."

The blessing was shared many times over. Ron and his wife, Paula, came to our church for many years after that, and they told quite a few others about their time at our home and how the Lord had moved in all of our lives.

The first couple years of the renovation went fast. Finally, enough had been completed for us to move in. Originally we'd planned to finish the renovations entirely before moving in, but we decided that living in the house would allow us to save money by not paying rent elsewhere, and being on site all the time would allow us to spend more time working on it, which would make the project go faster.

> Now to him who is able to do immeasurably more than all we ask or imagine, according to his power that is at work within us, to him be glory in the church and in Christ Jesus throughout all generations, for ever and ever!
>
> —EPHESIANS 3:20–21 (NIV)

It was the right decision. Our son, Aaron, came along about a month before we made the move. It was then that we realized we needed to slow down and rest for a while. We would calculate the cost of the next thing we wanted to do, and then spend several weeks saving up. Once the money ran out, we would spend a few more months saving before the next task.

> **Commit to the LORD whatever you do, and he will establish your plans.**
>
> —PROVERBS 16:3 (NIV)

Along the way, people at church or work would always ask how things were going. We lived in a small community, so everyone could see the progress when we were working on the outside, but now that we were on the inside only, they had to stop and visit to find out what we were up to. It always surprised us when our doorbell would ring and someone would be standing there asking if we were working today. If we had the materials, we were working, and if people had time, they would help us do what needed to be done. We were profoundly grateful not only for the way that the house was coming together but the spiritual fellowship happening between the people who were brought together during the process.

We were aware of God's hand on us from the first day to the last. When we couldn't accomplish a task, He brought us the ones who could. We were assured at every turn that the Father was with us and that it was His desire for us to not only succeed but to also be a blessing and be blessed during the process.

Finally, 8 years after we began, the last project was completed. It was the pouring of our driveway. As I watched the

GOD'S GIFT OF TASTE
— Heidi Gaul —

SWEET, SALTY, BITTER, sour, and umami (savory). These five basic flavors make up the spectrum of tastes we perceive with our tongue. Current research shows the tongue also has receptors that taste fat, making it likely it will soon be added to the existing flavor list. Why did God create so many flavors? Because He is a God of possibilities. He delights in our wonder at even the simplest of things. Like a beloved father at a backyard barbeque, He looks at all of us, His children, our "plates" and hearts full, and He is well-pleased.

---

workers building the braces that were to hold the concrete and pouring the liquid into it, I was reminded of how God had built the foundation of our home and our lives during those 8 years.

Today it has been more than 40 years since we began that restoration project, and we still run into people who tell stories of how God worked in their lives as they helped in ours. Looking back, we can still feel the impact of the love that was shown to us. God used friends, church family, relatives, and neighbors to help us not only in the restoration of a home but also in building relationships with Him. He was with us every step of the way and we could see Him in each one that came.

A Second Chance
Felicia Harris-Russell

"I know it looks bad, Ms. Felicia, but if you give me a chance, I promise I won't let you down." Tiara, a candidate for a customer service position in the call center I managed, made this promise to me during our interview.

Tiara arrived for our interview professionally dressed and presented herself as a bright, articulate, and respectful young woman. However, there was a major red flag with Tiara—her résumé showed several gaps in her employment history. During my managerial training, I had learned that gaps in employment history was a reason to immediately discard a résumé. Periods where a person didn't have a job were problematic because conventional wisdom said it showed the person was unstable and uncommitted—not at all desirable characteristics when searching for candidates to fill an open position. A résumé like Tiara's was expected to be tossed into the sea of forgetfulness, never to be recovered.

When I asked her about her employment gaps during the interview, Tiara provided plausible explanations. But was she being truthful, or had she found a job site online that told candidates the "right" answers to those questions?

I had doubts. But when Tiara made that promise not to let me down, a glowing sense of peace swirled inside me. It felt like someone was injecting warm, liquid honey—or perhaps a generous portion of angelic love—into my innermost being. Within seconds, my mind was completely changed, and I went from being a skeptic of Tiara to a fan. I didn't want to deny her. I believed her. I wanted her to win. I wanted to give Tiara a chance to prove herself and turn her life around. I wanted to fight for her.

Fighting was precisely what I would have to do. Every person I wanted to hire needed the approval of my supervisor, the director of the call center. Because I collaborated closely with him during the hiring process, I knew firsthand that in the past he had rejected résumés like Tiara's without hesitation.

This meant that if I, as a newly hired manager, decided to move forward with her candidacy, I would be risking my reputation. I would be jeopardizing my good standing in the company to advance the cause of a total stranger whose actions—if we hired her—would reflect directly on me. Did I want to put my own job at risk to give her a chance?

> **The steadfast love of the LORD never ceases; his mercies never come to an end; they are new every morning; great is your faithfulness.**
>
> —LAMENTATIONS 3:22–23 (ESV)

My heart was sending me a different message. It reminded me that I was once Tiara. There used to be gaps in the employment history on my résumé, too.

As an imperfect human, I've made my share of mistakes. In my younger years, I made quite a few decisions based on my feelings in the moment instead of taking time to think and use common sense, pray, or talk the situation over with someone wiser. Conflict resolution was not something I embraced. I was driven by pride and a temperamental disposition. Instead of staying and trying to find solutions to uncomfortable or difficult situations at work, I left. *I don't have to deal with this. I'll find another job,* I assured myself. Sometimes I quit abruptly without having another job lined up.

I had been a sociology major in college, and so I recognized my response as what is called *"fight or flight"*—a physiological response to a scary or threatening situation. Your instincts take over and you feel an overwhelming urge to either stay and fight or run away. I could identify the issue from an intellectual perspective, even as I watched myself back away from negative experiences, but I felt powerless to do anything about it. I lived a decade as a captive of this syndrome, which had a costly effect on many areas of my life, including relationships. I will forever be grateful to a church member named Deborah, a psychotherapist and Christian counselor, who started a weekly support group for women in our church. When we met, we prayed fervently for each other, and lovingly listened as we shared our past traumas, feelings of shame, and mistakes in a safe and non-judgmental environment. It was there that I discovered the root cause of why I ran, and it was there that my freedom from this syndrome began.

There will always be new things for me to learn in life, but thankfully, I've gained a little understanding along the way. I've learned that life is not always neat and orderly. Sometimes it seems like a lab experiment gone wrong, where good people can make bad decisions they later regret. And sometimes you must stay and work through your problems instead of retreating and running.

Far superior to any of those lessons, though, are the truths I've learned about God's grace and mercy. He desires the absolute best for each of us. His grace is truly amazing and always available to us in our time of need. And His mercy is all about second chances.

Now, sitting here with a woman who doubtless had been through her own learning experiences, I had an opportunity to pay forward the risk that someone had taken on me years before.

Who doesn't need mercy at some point in their lives? I thought to myself. The well-known phrase *"justice tempered with mercy"* has always had a special meaning for me, because it describes judgment that has been softened with kindness. It recognizes that anyone can make a mistake. I so appreciate the wisdom and compassion that lie in those four words.

> **For judgment is without mercy to one who has shown no mercy. Mercy triumphs over judgment.**
>
> —JAMES 2:13 (ESV)

I hired Tiara with my director's blessing. She proved to be one of the best employees I've ever had. She was hungry for success and won many center-wide contests. She was assigned several leadership roles within the department and was even allowed to participate in selecting new customer service representatives. On a personal level, being able to celebrate with her when she became a first-time homeowner brought me special joy.

When I left the company, Tiara was still there, thriving as a valued member of the team. Thanks to the divine nudge I received, she was able to keep her promise—she didn't let me down.

Contributors

Robin Ayscue   p. 186
Laura Bailey   p. 54
Rhoda Blecker   p. 155
Sharon Beth Brani   p. 77
Rachel Britton   p. 68
Tez Brooks   pp. 1, 21, 37, 81
Elizabeth Brown   p. 73
Leone F. Byron   p. 139
Patricia Cameron   pp. 83, 231
Elsa Kok Colopy   pp. 134, 163
Laurie Davies   p. 12
Sara Etgen-Baker   p. 47
Valorie Bridges Fant   p. 150
Heidi Gaul   p. 239
Deb Gorman   p. 127
Miriam Green   p. 214
Felicia Harris-Russell   p. 240
Jeannie Hughes   p. 203
Laurie Jeron   p. 63
Angela J. Kaufman   p. 144
Sharon Kirby   p. 18
Wendy Klopfenstein   p. 225
Marlene Kropf   p. 182
Linda L. Kruschke   pp. 97, 197
Lisa Livezey   p. 159

Erin Lynum   p. 126, 185
Sue McCusker   p. 42
Margaret McNeil   p. 58
Roberta Messner   pp. 122, 210
Renee Mitchell   pp. 93, 235
Pamela Montgomery   p. 176
Ana Arreola Moore   p. 168
Alice H. Murray   p. 199
Karen Register   p. 54
Betty A. Rodgers-Kulich   p. 23
Lori Stanley Roeleveld   p. 98
Maggie Willem Rowe
Diana DeSpain Schramer   p. 107
Kimberly Shumate   p. 61, 224
Susan Shumway   p. 194
Lorna Skylar   p. 33
Kathleen Stauffer   p. 190
Lori Rowe Summer   p. 88
B. J. Taylor   p. 116
Terrie Todd   pp. 142, 154
Marilyn Turk   p. 38
Linda VanderWeir   pp. 28, 219
Renee Yancy   p. 103

Acknowledgments

Every attempt has been made to credit the sources of copyrighted material used in this book. If any such acknowledgment has been inadvertently omitted or miscredited, receipt of such information would be appreciated.

Scripture quotations marked (ESV) are taken from *The Holy Bible, English Standard Version*. Copyright © 2001 by Crossway Bibles, a division of Good News Publishers. Used by permission. All rights reserved.

Scripture quotations marked (JPS) are taken from *Tanakh: A New Translation of the Holy Scriptures according to the Traditional Hebrew Text*. Copyright © 1985 by the Jewish Publication Society. All rights reserved.

Scripture quotations marked (KJV) are taken from the *King James Version of the Bible*.

Scripture quotations marked (NIV) are taken from *The Holy Bible, New International Version®, NIV®*. Copyright © 1973, 1978, 1984, 2011 by Biblica, Inc. Used by permission. All rights reserved worldwide.

Scripture quotations marked (NKJV) are taken from the *New King James Version®*. Copyright © 1982 by Thomas Nelson. Used by permission. All rights reserved.

Scripture quotations marked (NLT) are taken from the *Holy Bible, New Living Translation*. Copyright © 1996, 2004, 2007, 2015 by Tyndale House Foundation. Used by permission of Tyndale House Publishers Inc., Carol Stream, Illinois. All rights reserved.

Scripture quotations marked (NRSVUE) are taken from the *New Revised Standard Version, Updated Edition*. Copyright © 2021 National Council of Churches of Christ in the United States of America. Used by permission. All rights reserved worldwide.

A Note from the Editors

We hope you enjoyed *Angels & Divine Interventions,* published by Guideposts. For more than 75 years, Guideposts, a nonprofit organization, has been driven by a vision of a world filled with hope. We aspire to be the voice of a trusted friend, a friend who makes you feel more hopeful and connected.

By making a purchase from Guideposts, you join our community in touching millions of lives, inspiring them to believe that all things are possible through faith, hope, and prayer. Your continued support allows us to provide uplifting resources to those in need. Whether through our communities, websites, apps, or publications, we inspire our audiences, bring them together, and comfort, uplift, entertain, and guide them. Visit us at guideposts.org to learn more.

We would love to hear from you. Write us at Guideposts, P.O. Box 5815, Harlan, Iowa 51593 or call us at (800) 932-2145. Did you love *Angels & Divine Interventions*? Leave a review for this product on guideposts.org/shop. Your feedback helps others in our community find relevant products.

Find inspiration, find faith, find Guideposts.
Shop our best sellers and favorites at
guideposts.org/shop
Or scan the QR code to go directly to our Shop